I0797225

ALSO BY KEN REID

Ken Reid's Hometown Hockey Heroes

One to Remember: Stories from 39 Members of the NHL's One Goal Club

Dennis Maruk: The Unforgettable Story of Hockey's Forgotten 60-Goal Man (with Dennis Maruk)

One Night Only: Conversations with the NHL's One-Game Wonders

Hockey Card Stories 2: 59 More True Tales from Your Favourite Players

Hockey Card Stories: True Tales from Your Favourite Players

THE NEXT ONE

Hockey Scouts, Remote Rinks and Hidden Talent

KEN REID

Published by Simon & Schuster

NEW YORK AMSTERDAM/ANTWERP LONDON
TORONTO SYDNEY/MELBOURNE NEW DELHI

A Division of Simon & Schuster, LLC
166 King Street East, Suite 300
Toronto, Ontario M5A 1J3

This Simon & Schuster Canada edition October 2025

SIMON & SCHUSTER CANADA and colophon are trademarks of Simon & Schuster, LLC

Simon & Schuster strongly believes in freedom of expression and stands against censorship in all its forms. For more information, visit BooksBelong.com.

For information about special discounts for bulk purchases, please contact Simon & Schuster Special Sales at 1-800-268-3216 or CustomerService@simonandschuster.ca.

Manufactured in the United States of America

1 3 5 7 9 10 8 6 4 2

Online Computer Library Center number: 1492139268

ISBN 978-1-6680-4558-9
ISBN 978-1-6680-4559-6 (ebook)

To my sons, Jacoby and Langdon.

Like a good scout, always keep your eyes, ears and minds open.

With love, Dad.

And to the family and friends of Gerry McNamara,

who passed away before the publishing of this book.

Thank you, Gerry, for your kindness.

Contents

CONTENTS

Foreword

Combine hockey—Canada's national pastime—with an unmatched pride in his country and an unmatched passion for this beloved pastime and you have Ken Reid. Ken's onscreen persona with his full-time gig at Sportsnet never failed to catch my eye, induce a head shake and belly laugh, and leave me in wonderment at where and when the on-air character gained its inception. It was only when I had the pleasure of meeting him in person, listening to his endless stories, observing his passion for collecting heartfelt memorabilia, embracing his East Coast gibberish, respecting his role as a husband and proud father, that I truly came to the realization: this is not an on-air character—this is Ken Reid.

Ken's passion for the sport of hockey, and all of the crazy and adventurous characters and tales that resonate as the sport continues to evolve, explore a topic that is so close to my heart and my personal experiences in the game—the role and passionate tales of a scout. The tireless travels through blizzards, ice storms, countless cancelled flights, rental cars, changing time zones, multiple visas, all in the pursuit of uncovering that hidden gem, the game changer, the missing piece that just might somehow provide your team with an advantage in that relentless pursuit of a championship.

Through his passion for the hockey industry, and a job description so personal to me, Ken articulates this tireless profession through the eyes of varying generations of those in pursuit of the next great talent. From hockey lifer and savant Paul Henry to the brilliant young hockey mind of current Ontario Hockey League manager James Boyd, he highlights the stories, relationships and bonds that are cherished in our seemingly endless hockey lore.

Ken, combining his thorough storytelling with his unique sense of humour, introduces the reader to a unique group, all filled with character and unmatched love for the sport of hockey. As the analytics gurus have infiltrated the art of the scout and the live-eye test, getting to the core soul of a player will come under scrutiny. Until we create a numerical equation to define the key ingredient of any individual's true will to succeed.

Character. There will always be a place in the corner of every chilly rink where the greatest game in the world is played for the hockey scout.

—Mike Futa, former assistant general manager for the Los Angeles Kings and two-time Stanley Cup champion

Introduction

It never fails. Whenever I go to a midget or junior hockey game, the first thing I do is look for a roster. For some reason, I want to play hockey scout. Just last week, my sons and I went to an Oshawa Generals–Barrie Colts game. Well, it turns out my two boys are the same as the old man.

"Give me the roster! Give me the roster!" shouted my oldest. I did what I was told. We immediately started scouring the players. The play began, and yep, soon enough, the old man was falling in love with a big Barrie defenceman. "Look at the size of that guy, kids," I said.

Now, I am by no means a scouting genius. This guy would stand out to anyone. If there's one thing I know, you can't teach size. This guy was big, mean and throwing his body around at will. So, we did what everybody does these days. We looked at his name on the roster, and then we googled him.

It turns out that Gabriel Eliasson is a second-round pick of the Ottawa Senators in the 2024 draft. Dad was no genius, but I could at least spot this guy.

I guess I picked up the bug a long time ago. My mom, Marie, and I used to do the same thing at Halifax Mooseheads games. We'd be watching players like Alex Tanguay and Jody Shelley, wondering if they had "it." Now my kids were doing the same thing with me.

"There he is," my youngest said to me. My boys wanted to check out another Barrie player, a six-foot-one, 198-pound defenceman, Kashawn Aitcheson. My oldest had the scoop on Kashawn. He at least knew he was a nice guy. Kashawn had stopped by to visit my son's Don Mills Flyers minor hockey team a couple of weeks earlier. I will give the kids credit. He is a good player. The boys liked what they saw, and so did I. Kashawn is ranked among the top sixty skaters in North America for the 2025 NHL draft.

Hockey fans across the planet play the same game my sons and I play. We all think we can spot the next big thing. We all, from time to time, play scout. And let's face it: most of us can spot the next big thing. It's easy to see the magic and potential of a teenage Sidney Crosby or Connor McDavid. But how do you go out and find a guy like Antoine Roussel? Roussel didn't average a point per game during his four-year junior career with the Chicoutimi Saguenéens. He wasn't drafted. But a scout—one in this book, in fact—saw something in the player, and he went on to play in over six hundred career regular-season NHL games. That's scouting.

But that's just one part of the book. My biggest question is: Who are the men and women who make up the hockey scouting community? That's what this book is all about. This book is not necessarily about what goes into scouting a player, although that's in here, too, but it is about what goes into the making of a scout.

Kevin Hanson from Simon & Schuster came up with the idea for this book. He figured that maybe I'd know a few scouts. And maybe those scouts would have a few stories they could share, about their winters spent in planes, trains and, yes, automobiles—and, of course, the rink.

Well, it turns out that Kevin's hunch was correct. In putting this book together, I've talked to a plethora of people from backgrounds I could not imagine. One of the scouts I talked to is a psychologist.

Another is a musician, another a farmer. There are a couple of referees in there, and, of course, ex-players, hockey lifers, who just can't get the smell of the rink and the glory of the game out of their veins.

I learned a lot putting this book together. For one, you have to continue to grow as a hockey scout, no matter how old-school you may be. You need to adjust with the times. And perhaps the number one thing I learned is that it is easy to fall in love with a player the first time you see them. Therefore, you have to see a player a certain number of times before you can fully commit to them—or, perhaps more importantly, not commit to them at all.

Sit back and enjoy these stories. Sure, they are hockey stories, but they are also people stories. I mean, how do you go from being a hockey-loving farmer to a scout who happens to own a farm? Imagine working at Millhaven maximum-security prison, and a few years later you're scouting for the New York Rangers. Or how about sharing a seat on a drive with Glenn Hall, one of the greatest hockey goalies of all time, to make it from a Toronto Marlboros junior game out to Belleville, and by the end of the drive you haven't heard endless stories from Hall but you at least got a song out of it.

And by the end of this book, you will no doubt learn the most universal scouting creed: There are no bad scouts, only bad . . .

THE NEXT ONE

CHAPTER 1

The Original Swedish Adventure

Gerry McNamara

Hockey Hall of Famer Börje Salming and Gerry McNamara share a moment years after the old Leafs scout first laid eyes on Börje in late 1972. COURTESY GERRY McNAMARA

"The highlight of my career was finding Börje," says Gerry McNamara. McNamara was in his late eighties when he recalled his greatest hockey adventure. McNamara has pretty much done and seen it all. He played junior with Frank Mahovlich. A few years after that, he played in the Original Six era for the Toronto Maple Leafs. In the late 1970s he coached the top farm team for the Leafs and the Chicago Black Hawks. In the 1980s he had an eight-year run as the general manager of the Leafs. But the highlight of his career was finding Hockey Hall of Fame defenceman Börje Salming. He told me, "Salming is the best defenceman who ever played in the National Hockey League. Nobody had moves like him, and if anybody is doubting what I'm saying, I always say to them, go back and look at films and see some of the moves. The guy was unbelievable."

McNamara first saw Salming in late December 1972. But his journey to that point had started years earlier.

McNamara was in the same boat as a lot of great hockey players in the 1950s and 1960s. That boat was called the minor leagues. With only six teams in the NHL, jobs in the game's top league were at a premium. It was even tougher to crack the NHL when you were a goalie. The six teams each carried just one goaltender. When McNamara was a young pro, there was no such thing as a permanent backup. He came about as close as you could in 1958, when the Leafs loaned McNamara to the Detroit Red Wings to back up Terry Sawchuk for the playoffs. McNamara knew a couple of the Red Wings, Bill Dineen and Al Arbour. He also knew the trainer, Lefty Wilson. "Those three guys were the only three guys who spoke to me when I went to Detroit. Not one of the other players ever came up to say 'welcome' or 'Gerry, we're glad you're here.' Sawchuk, Howe, you name it. None of them did. It's boiled into my mind. If I was a veteran and some kid came in like that, and I was just a kid, you could come over and shake their hand and say welcome. I might have had to play goal for them! It was crazy. But that was the National Hockey League back then."

A couple of seasons later, McNamara finally got his chance. He was playing for Sudbury of the old Eastern Professional Hockey League when he got the call from the Leafs. "Johnny Bower got hurt. They needed a goalie," he said.

Gerry played in Maple Leaf Gardens against Jean Béliveau and the Montreal Canadiens on February 15, 1961. Boom Boom Geoffrion and Doug Harvey played for the Habs too. Jacques Plante was their goaltender. The Leafs had a lineup that featured Frank Mahovlich, Allan Stanley and Tim Horton. Unlike the Wings, the Leafs all talked to their goalie. The Canadiens won the game, 3–1. "It was something I was waiting for, for a pretty long time. I thought I played pretty well when I got up there. I thought I played well enough that they should have kept me for the next year. I don't think much about it now; I had my chance and I played well. I was happy with the way I played."

McNamara got into a total of five games with the Leafs during the 1960–61 season. But then it was back to the minors. "I quit December 15, 1963. I got hurt. I was playing for the Charlotte Checkers, and I got hurt in Philadelphia. I didn't play again in the Eastern League. Around mid-January or the first of February, I told the team, 'I don't think I can play anymore. Just give me a plane ticket and the rest of my money.' I came home."

But the game wasn't finished with McNamara; far from it. He worked at a number of jobs while playing senior hockey at the same time. He even had a brief comeback with the Leafs when he played two games for the club in the 1969–70 season, and then a few years later the Leafs would call again. He was working as an equipment representative for Winnwell when the Maple Leafs called his house in September 1972. General manager Jim Gregory was looking for a scout. McNamara set up a meeting.

"I went down to see Jimmy. He offered me a scouting job. Jimmy and I knew each other for a long time," says Gerry. They were both grads of St. Michael's College School. McNamara was still playing senior hockey when he was offered the job. "I was hired at the beginning of the exhibition season. I played a game in Barrie on September 21, and we beat them. It was an exhibition game. The next thing I knew, I was with the Maple Leafs. That was the last game I played."

Gregory and the Leafs didn't have any advice for the new hire about how to be a scout. McNamara figured he did have one advantage. "I do have a theory. I've said this a few times: goaltenders make the best scouts. Goaltenders see the whole picture. They have a panoramic view. They see everything that's going on. You see the good passers, the bad passers. You even become a referee, too, you're calling the lines. I really believe that being a goaltender gave me a great start. Nobody sat me down and said, 'You scout this way, or you scout that way' when I went to Toronto."

The Leafs may have not told McNamara how to scout, but they did tell him where he would be scouting. "Jimmy said, 'I'm going to make you our special assignment scout. I'm going to send you wherever I want to send you. You'll go to the International Hockey League. You'll go into the American League.' And that's what I did. The big deal came on December 27, 1972, when I flew over to Sweden."

And that was the most special assignment, the one that would make him a part of hockey lore. In fact, it would even make him a part of a television series, with Jason Priestley playing the role of a young Gerry McNamara in *Börje*. "I thought he did a great job. I got to meet him. I really liked him. He was kind to me. I thought he did a good job. The only difference is that I'm a little taller than him . . . but that's okay," Gerry chuckles.

On the world stage, Sweden was not a complete hockey unknown in 1972. The Swedes had won bronze medals at the two previous World Hockey Championships. Before that, they had won back-to-back silver medals. As for scouting in Sweden, it was much different. McNamara did not have much competition. "I had the whole country to myself. There was not one NHL scout there except for me."

Think about it this way: If Swedish hockey was an all-you-can-eat buffet, McNamara had the whole restaurant to himself. And there wasn't a lineup outside the restaurant, either. No one else was coming. It was like no one else even knew about it. What might the rest of the NHL have thought if they'd heard of the Leafs sending a scout to Sweden? "They likely thought we were off our rocker," says McNamara, who was just thirty-eight years old when he made the trip.

The initial purpose of McNamara's trip was to check out a goaltender named Curt Larsson. He went and watched Larsson play for his club team, Södertälje SK: "He was good, but I didn't think he was better than what we had," says Gerry. The Leafs at the time had Bernie Parent as their number one goalie, an aging Jacques Plante was the backup, and Ron Low was the Leafs' top minor-league goalie. (Larsson ended up playing for the Winnipeg Jets in the World Hockey Association. He played sixty-eight games over three seasons with a 4.16 goals-against average.) McNamara told Gregory what he thought of Larsson. Gregory then told Gerry that there were a couple of tournaments on the go in Sweden and he should check out a few other teams.

McNamara wasn't looking for a goalie anymore, but he was looking for someone. He just didn't know who. He *did* know what type of player he wanted. "I had some points that I had in my head on what a player has to do to get my attention. Of course, the number one thing is skating. If you're not a very good skater, I'll sort of pass you by."

McNamara checked out a game that involved a team called Brynäs. They were in Division I, which was then Sweden's highest league, and that's when Gerry McNamara found just the player he was looking for.

"When I saw Börje on the ice, he was unbelievable. I never saw anything like it before in the National Hockey League and I've never seen anything like it since. The guy was unbelievable when I saw him in Sweden. And the first thing I said was 'We have to have him!' And then I watched him play a second game."

The second game was against the Barrie Flyers, a senior hockey team on a tour of Sweden. McNamara knew the team and some of their players very well. He had been picked up by the Flyers the previous season for their run to the Allan Cup, and the last game he ever played, just a few months earlier, had been against the Flyers. In short, he knew who these guys were and what they were going to try to do to Börje. McNamara took his seat.

"The Canadians, they think they're going to run the Swedes out of the rink. That's the mentality that they had. Börje didn't back off. He gave it right back. As soon as I saw that from Börje, I thought, *He's got it all. He's got courage and he certainly has the skating and ability.* He was unbelievable. He scored two goals and Inge Hammarström scored five against Barrie."

If McNamara wasn't already convinced about Salming's courage, he got a little bonus late in the game. With about three minutes to go, Salming got into a fight. When he left the ice, Börje skated right by McNamara. The Leafs scout knew what he had to do. He got up out of his seat and headed for Salming's dressing room. When he got to the door, the trainer answered. Salming was the only player in the room. McNamara was only steps away from a private audience with his now-prized prospect. "I said to the trainer, 'I'd like to speak with Börje.' I could see Börje sitting on the bench in the dressing room. And Börje didn't say this when he told this story; he always said, 'I don't know how you got in the room!' But I got in the room because Börje told the trainer to get out."

With the trainer gone, McNamara made his move. He stepped in front of the lanky defenceman, a kid he had only seen play twice, and did his thing. "I just showed Börje my card. I said, 'I'm Gerry McNamara. I scout for the Toronto Maple Leafs. You can play for the Toronto Maple Leafs. Are you interested?'"

Salming didn't speak great English at the time. He suggested to McNamara that he speak to Hammarström. That was fine with Gerry. He had his eye on the Swedish sniper, too. Soon enough, the game ended. "I left my card with Börje. I left the room. I waited for the team to come off the ice and I went up to Inge and I told him the same thing. And he said yes, he was interested. I said, 'Okay, we will be in touch with you guys.'"

McNamara and the Leafs didn't immediately pursue Salming and Hammarström. These days, any free-agent find would be pursued non-stop. But this was 1972. And Salming and Hammarström were in Sweden. As Gerry said, there wasn't another NHL scout in the country. If you're wondering if McNamara went away in a ball of stress, praying and hoping that his secret pair would not be found by somebody else, the answer is no. In 1972 if you were in Europe and found a hot prospect, you didn't have to sign him. You just had to put him on your team's negotiation list. If you did that, no other NHL team could sign that player. So, they put Salming and Hammarström on their negotiation list. (The WHA was around, but not in the picture at this point.) The Leafs didn't attempt to have Salming and Hammarström sign contracts until they saw them in Moscow in April 1973 at the World Hockey Championships.

And when McNamara made the trip to that tournament, he had more than just Salming and Hammarström in mind. Two other Swedish players were on his negotiation list: future WHA superstar Anders Hedberg and Willy Lindström. McNamara wasn't alone on this trip; Bob Davidson, the Leafs' head scout, also made the trip to the Soviet Union for the championships. "Bob had gone over with me, I guess to check and see whether I knew what I was talking about," McNamara recalls.

The first player the pair was set to deal with was Hedberg, who would go on to be part of the most productive line in WHA history—the Winnipeg Jets' Hot Line, which also included Ulf Nilsson and Bobby Hull. Hedberg was incredible in the WHA, where he put up 458 points in 256 regular-season games. He played another 465 games in the NHL, with the New York Rangers, and scored 398 points. That's 856 points in 721 North American major-league games. McNamara knew he had someone special when Hedberg knocked on the door of his hotel room. Davidson? Not so much.

"Anders came up to our room, and the first thing—and as soon as it happened, I thought, *We're dead.*—Bob said to Anders, 'What makes you think you can play in the National Hockey League?' That's the worst thing you can say to a Swede. Believe me, the worst thing! I went in with a positive view with Börje and Inge and it worked. It worked perfectly. And I never got a word out of my mouth with Anders. When Bob asked his question, I could see the look on Anders' face. And my heart went right up into my throat. I knew we had no chance, and that's exactly what happened."

Nor did the Leafs get Lindström, who would score 584 points in

898 games between the WHA and NHL, winning two Stanley Cups with the Edmonton Oilers.

Just imagine if the Leafs had signed Anders Hedberg! Salming and Hedberg on the Leafs, along with Darryl Sittler and Lanny McDonald. "I know Hedberg would've been really good, too, and if we would've gotten him with the Maple Leafs, I tell you something, the Leafs, we were on our way."

But McNamara did get Salming and Hammarström for the Leafs. They finally signed that June. In his first year on the job, Gerry had landed two big fish.

"People ask me all the time: 'You were just starting as a scout. How did you feel when you put these guys on your negotiation list? Were you nervous?' To be honest, no. I didn't have any nerves at all about that. I just used my own judgment. I thought I was a good assessor of players even before I started to scout. I always thought that I had a good eye for the game."

Salming and Hammarström arrived in Toronto a couple of weeks before the Maple Leafs' 1973 training camp. Salming was coming off a World Championship where he had been the highest-scoring defenceman and had been named to the tournament's All-Star team. Hammarström, who was twenty-five, three years older than Salming, had nine points in ten games at the worlds. Still, there were doubters.

"The head coach, Johnny McLellan, told me, 'You better be right, Mac.' And Bob Davidson would be sitting there when we were discussing the players and he wouldn't say a word. He never said, 'Gerry, don't worry. You're right.' He was the chief scout and I never remember once where he backed me up to say, 'Don't worry, they can play.' He never said that once, and that's the honest-to-goodness truth. And it hurt me. But I went to Johnny McLellan and I said, 'I'm going to tell you something: Börje Salming is going to be a superstar in the National Hockey League. Mark my words.'"

When McNamara met the pair in Toronto, he told them there was ice available at the Gardens if they wanted to skate. The Swedes took McNamara up on his offer. McNamara and a few of the Leafs brass were in the stands when the pair took to the Gardens ice for the first time. "Börje and Inge got together, and Börje said, 'Let's really show them. Let's put on a show for them.'"

McNamara looked at the faces of Leafs owner Harold Ballard, Davidson, McLellan and anyone else who happened to be lucky enough to be at the rink that day. He could see the look of amazement on their faces as they watched the pair on the ice. "When they saw Börje and Inge come out on the ice that day, when they saw the way they skated, the way they handled the puck . . . and the way they shot the puck! And it was just the two of them," McNamara chuckles. "Börje and Inge did indeed put a show on, and it was to my benefit. I said, 'I told you they're good players. Don't worry about them.' I never, ever thought, *Oh, I hope they're good enough*. I never ever had that thought in my mind."

Even with the show the Swedish duo put on that day, doubt still lingered. Remember, only a chosen few had seen Salming and Hammarström skate. When training camp began, the Swedish pair were the story, and whether they could really play was the question to be answered. "I'm out here to see if Gerry McNamara is as good a scout as he claims he is," Johnny Bower told the *Toronto Star*. (Knowing Bower, he may have said this with a bit of a smirk on his face.) "I'm going to play goal against his Swedes," the retired Bower said, "and see if they deserve the rating [Gerry] gave them on his report."

Bower's verdict after he shared the ice with Salming and Hammarström and faced a bevy of shots? "They are good. Will be great if they can stand up to the heavy body contact, which is a big part of the National Hockey League. They are fine skaters, pass and handle the puck expertly and are smart around the net. They stay far enough out to prevent a goalkeeper from using a poke check when shooting on goal, and they keep their heads up, so they don't have to look down to see where the puck is. They could feel it on their sticks, know when it is in position and make a shot or pass."

Many people wondered about that "heavy body contact." The Leafs opened their season at home against the Buffalo Sabres and won, 7–4. Salming picked up his first NHL point when he assisted on a Darryl Sittler goal. The next night, on October 11, 1973, was the test a lot of doubters were waiting for. The Leafs went to Philly to take on the Flyers. These were the Broad Street Bullies, a team that would wreak havoc on the NHL in that 1973–74 season, ultimately winning the Cup that spring. The team had its share of heavies—Dave "The Hammer" Schultz, Don Saleski, Bob Kelly and more. They were led by head coach Fred Shero, who made no apologies for this team's dog-on-a-bone mentality. "You can't believe the punishment that he took in his first year. Philadelphia was brutal," recalls McNamara. "They were brutal. I blame Freddy Shero. I don't blame anybody else but Freddy Shero. I'm sure that he sent those guys out on the ice to go and do whatever they could do to Börje."

Following that first game in Philly, *Toronto Star* reporter Red Burnett wrote about the abuse Salming had had to put up with. "Börje Salming, Maple Leafs rookie defenceman, is earning the respect of National Hockey League rivals which in his case is most important. It was obvious the league's badmen would challenge the Swedish import to see if he could stand the tough going. Their efforts have been crude, and in some cases brutal, but the 6′1″ 185 pounder from Kiruna, Sweden, has not backed off an inch."

The Flyers were just playing the way Shero wanted them to play. They played mean, like a pack of mad dogs. If one Flyer was attacked, everyone on the team considered themselves to be under attack. McNamara says Shero the coach was night-and-day different from Shero the player. "I played with Freddy Shero," says McNamara. "I could tell you I never saw Freddy Shero hit anybody. So, I'm just saying that's my opinion. And those guys all learned to respect Börje. Everybody in the National Hockey League learned to respect Börje."

How did Salming do it? How did he take the abuse? What made him tough enough? "First of all, Börje had an unbelievable body. He didn't have an ounce of fat on him," begins McNamara. He then points out where Börje grew up: a small village called Salmi, now in the municipality of Kiruna, in northern Sweden, where the winters are long and harsh. Börje's father died in a mining accident when he was only five years old. "He had a tough life when he was growing up," McNamara says. "Apparently, there used to be gangs after him. He took some beatings . . . but when he became a hockey player, I'll tell you right now, he didn't back up an inch. I was in the dressing room one night after a game in Philadelphia, and his skin looked like a pin cushion. The spearing he took . . . it was unspeakable."

Börje Salming became a superstar in Toronto and the NHL almost instantly. And Gerry McNamara was proven to be more than correct on his big Swedish hunch. He still thinks the Leafs should have gotten more out of Inge Hammarström, too. "I really believe that the Toronto Maple Leafs mishandled Inge. Roger Neilson was a defensive coach and he talked Jimmy [Gregory] into trading Inge to the St. Louis Blues for Jerry Butler, who was just a defensive player. He couldn't carry Inge's jock. Inge scored twenty goals each year he played with the Maple Leafs [he scored twenty, twenty-one, nineteen and twenty-four in his four full seasons with the Leafs], and he played on the third and fourth lines. He never played on the first or second line. If he had, I really believe he would've scored thirty goals, or even thirty-five or forty. That's how good he was."

The Hammarström trade was part of the debacle that began when Harold Ballard got deeper into his reign as Maple Leafs owner. He traded Inge, he traded Tiger Williams, he traded Lanny McDonald. Ballard traded everyone. Except for Börje Salming.

Early in the 1981–82 season, Gerry McNamara took over as the team's acting general manager, after Punch Imlach suffered a health scare. McNamara eventually was named GM, and was in the post until he was fired on February 7, 1988. Ballard presided over a lot of things during that decade. He even hired and fired the coaches. But he did not control the draft—or the scouting. "When I got fired, they said, 'He's no good,' the whole bit. But I can tell you right now, later on when they finally found the players and saw the players I put on the ice and they started to gain some traction, people started to change. And now I don't hear anybody say, 'He did a rotten job.' I hear people say, 'You know, he did a really good job. We saw who he drafted.'"

In 2024, Gerry can still rattle off the names from the 1987 draft, his final one as the Leafs' general manager. "I thought I was a really good scout and knew what I was talking about. Some of my last picks? Luke Richardson, Daniel Marois, John McIntyre, Joe Sacco, Damian Rhodes and Mike Eastwood. They all played in the National Hockey League. That's not a bad record."

There were some other great picks over the years as well—Wendel Clark, Al Iafrate, Russ Courtnall, Vincent Damphousse, Todd Gill and Gary Leeman. But there was only one Börje Salming. The one that Gerry McNamara discovered when he was all alone, almost at the North Pole.

The hockey world lost Börje Salming on November 24, 2022, when he died of amyotrophic lateral sclerosis (ALS).

"I phoned him one day and he didn't answer. I thought, 'Well, he must be really busy.' And then I got an email from Börje, and he wrote me 'I can't speak.' I didn't know that he was sick," says Gerry. "I didn't know that at the time. When he said, 'I can't speak,' I thought he must be tied up with somebody. But then I found out that he had ALS. He literally couldn't speak."

Two weeks before he died, Börje Salming was honoured by the Maple Leafs. On Friday, November 11, 2022, Salming and a group of other Hall of Famers were celebrated by the Leafs on the Hockey Hall of Fame's induction weekend. With fellow Swede Mats Sundin to his left and Darryl Sittler to his right, Salming heard the applause of the Toronto crowd. His old captain, Sittler, in tears, raised Börje's right arm to salute the crowd.

Then Salming raised his left arm and waved on his own.

The next night, Salming stood at centre ice at Scotiabank Arena. Once again, there was not a dry eye in the arena. Salming, surrounded by his family this time, burst into tears. Tears were everywhere in Scotiabank Arena on both nights. For whatever reason, the Leafs did not invite McNamara. "I can't believe they didn't invite me. I can't believe they didn't invite Inge. That's part of hockey. That's part of history. And I can't believe they didn't do that."

McNamara says he has since patched things up with the Leafs and is now a part of their alumni association. He was not at the arena that weekend to honour history, but he is part of it. There's lots of proof. Just turn on your TV. McNamara says the TV series *Börje* has changed his life. "I'm back . . . after twenty-five years of hibernation."

One of the scenes in the series shows the incredible ovation the Maple Leaf Gardens crowd gave Börje when he played for Sweden against Canada in the 1976 Canada Cup. By that time, he had won the hearts of Toronto fans. "I had tears in my eyes watching it. And when I think of it, I admit it, I still get tears in my eyes. That's how important Börje was to me. He did a lot more for me than I ever did for him."

Gerry McNamara passed away on April 11, 2025.

In a social media post the day after his death, the Maple Leafs said, "Gerry made an enduring impact on the organization, most notably by bringing Börje Salming to Toronto, helping pave the way for future generations of European players in the NHL."

CHAPTER 2

All in the Family

Brad Davis

Brad Davis learned everything he knew from his father, Lorne. He often went toe to toe with one of the game's greatest scouts, his father. COURTESY BRAD DAVIS

It's a natural thing, really. A lot of kids want to do what their dads do. If you grow up with your dad on a farm, maybe you'll become a farmer one day as well. If your mom or dad is a doctor, maybe you'll become a doctor. The same goes for just about every profession, including hockey scout. "In my mind, I was always going to be a scout," says former Edmonton Oilers scout Brad Davis.

Brad was the youngest son of Lorne Davis, a long-time Oilers bird dog who played over fifteen years of professional hockey. He won a Stanley Cup with the Montreal Canadiens. He shared the ice with hockey legends—and shared a dressing room with countless teammates, including Rocket Richard, Gordie Howe, Ted Lindsay, Terry Sawchuk and, during his time with the American Hockey League's Hershey Bears, Don Cherry.

"Dad was the best storyteller," says Brad. He first started hearing stories from his dad around the kitchen table as a kid in Regina, Saskatchewan. Years later, he'd hear the same stories from his dad while they scouted together with the Oilers. "I'd sit in the passenger seat or in the driver's seat, whichever seat it was, and give Dad that little plant, a little seed to get the story out of Dad that I wanted to hear. I probably heard the story ten times, but I wanted to hear the newest version."

His favourite? "It's probably a heartbreaking one. Every time I see Don Cherry he says, 'The Cocoa Inn!'"

You can still stay at the Cocoa Inn if you ever want to spend a night in Hershey, Pennsylvania. Once upon a time, Lorne Davis and his wife, Shirley, lived there, along with Hershey Bears teammate Don Cherry and his wife, Rose. "I walk my dog and everyone says, 'Oh,

Don Cherry's dog!' and I say, 'Yeah. My dad used to live with him.' I have the same type of bull terrier that Don has.

"Dad had this old story. There was a player who was on their team in Hershey who only played at home. This player was married to a European girl who was a real pretty girl, but he was running around on her. Whenever Dad and Don had to go to the train station to head out for a road game, this player would have his suitcase packed and he would hop in the car with Dad and Don and kiss his wife goodbye. She would think he was going to catch the train or the bus, just like Dad and Don were going to do down in Harrisburg [the team travelled out of Harrisburg], but then the other girl would pick this guy up in Harrisburg. And off they would go until the team came home from the road."

Davis can only imagine the conversation this guy would have with his wife when the Bears finally pulled back into Hershey. "'Yeah, yeah. I didn't play again. I didn't get in the lineup,'" Brad surmises.

Brad Davis grew up hearing countless stories like that from his father. They added a little colour to the game. He also sat around hearing of the qualities of this player or that player. When scouts were heading through Regina, they would visit the Davis house, and young Brad would sit in on the conversation they had with Lorne, discussing the virtues of hundreds of NHL prospects. He was getting his education. Davis took the long road to start his scouting career. He may not have known it as a kid, but all that time spent with his father was his hockey education. Like a young boy watching his dad farm a field, Brad was getting an up-close perspective on his future vocation.

• • •

In Regina he was Lorne's kid. Sure, as a young player that came with pressure. Lorne played in the NHL, so Brad was expected to be a solid player as well. But the fact that Lorne was Brad's dad also had its benefits.

In 1981, the St. Louis Blues held their training camp in Regina. They were set to play the Edmonton Oilers in an exhibition game. The night before the game, the young Oilers—hot off a playoff upset against the Montreal Canadiens just a few months earlier—gathered at the Davis house. Mark Messier was there. Andy Moog was there. A few others were there. And the man in charge of the whole thing, head coach and general manager Glen Sather, was there as well. "They said to me, 'You're coming out to practice in the morning, right?'"

Sadly, Davis knew a no from his mother was on the way. He was just starting high school, and the next day was a school day. "My mom was serious about school and responsibility and accountability. The family didn't work without my mom."

But his mom, Shirley, knew what was in front of her young son. Her answer shocked him. "I remember her saying to Glen, 'Yeah, of course he's coming to practice.' I didn't know whether to shit or steal. That wasn't my mom at all, but she recognized this opportunity that I was going to get to practise [with the Oilers]."

The next morning, Brad Davis was one of the first to hit the ice for practice at Regina's Agridome (now the Brandt Centre). The next thing he knew, a young Grant Fuhr was on the ice with him.

Then the NHL's toughest man came skating up to Brad. Davis knew Dave Semenko well. At least, he knew *of* him. Brad had been the stick boy for his dad's junior team a few years before, and Lorne and Dave went at it one night, right there on the bench. Now Davis was sharing the ice with Big Dave. Semenko told him to head off the ice and get a practice jersey. Brad did what he was told. He figured that Oilers equipment man Lyle "Sparky" Kulchinsky would be just off the ice, ready to hand him a practice jersey. Sparky wasn't there, but someone else was. "There is Wayne Gretzky, holding this red jersey for me to put on, a practice jersey. Then it took me a few laps before I realized, 'Holy shit! Gretzky has a red jersey on, too! I think I'm playing the wing with Wayne today!'"

The kid was right. He got to practise on Wayne Gretzky's line. "Curt Brackenbury was our other winger. I probably shouldn't say this, but I think Wayne was happy to have me on the one side," Davis laughs. Brackenbury definitely would have been the muscle on that line. As for how things went playing alongside number 99? "There I am, practising with Wayne Gretzky doing drills. I never had the balls to go to the net in my life, but I did at practice that day. It went just like everybody thought it would go. If you went to the net with your stick down, it was amazing what would happen."

Davis can't remember much more from the practice. Just the jersey, the ease of playing with Wayne and the smell of Polo cologne in the Oilers room after things wrapped up. The next day, Davis did what any ordinary kid would do, he went to school. When he walked into his algebra class, his teacher, Dennis Pottage, was waiting for him. Aside from being a teacher, Pottage was also one of Saskatchewan's top hockey officials. He is now a member of the Saskatchewan Sports Hall of Fame. On October 1, 1981, though, he was Mr. Pottage the algebra teacher. And he wanted to know why his young student had been absent the previous day.

"Where were you yesterday?"

Young Brad did not want to brag. He didn't want to belt out in front of the whole class that he had the best reason ever to miss school—that he had been practising with Wayne Gretzky. Davis decided to play it cool. He told his teacher, "There's a note in the office."

Mr. Pottage persisted. He kept asking Brad where he'd been. Brad stuck to his guns and kept repeating the same line: "There's a note in the office." When the bell rang, every young student's worst nightmare came true. When the kids started walking to the door, Mr. Pottage let out the dreaded words, "Everybody can go. Except Mr. Davis!"

The door closed. All the kids were gone. It was just Brad and Mr. Pottage. Trouble was on the way—a detention, maybe? No. It turns out Davis wasn't the only one who had played hooky the day before.

"Mr. Pottage said he and the other algebra teacher at school also skipped class in the morning to go watch practice. He said, 'We were wondering who the little guy in the Jofa on Gretzky's line was. We thought it might have been Keith Gretzky, but it didn't take long to figure out it was you.'"

That is a great teacher to have in your corner.

Davis had his hockey career cut short thanks to a couple of neck injuries. He played a little bit of junior and fractured the C6 vertebra in his neck, and then hurt it again. "I dove into a shallow pool right after breaking my neck and did the same thing again. I am lucky to be walking."

Brad's playing days were over. But he was still just a kid, a kid with a passion for hockey. How could he stay in the game? Simple. He could put on the stripes. The fact that his hockey-loving algebra teacher Mr. Pottage wore the stripes did not hurt, either. Davis's ascension up the referee ranks was fast. "Mr. Pottage and I ended up working lines in the Western Hockey League. One moment he was teaching me Grade 12, and the next thing I knew, we were working the lines together."

Brad Davis was a 170-pound kid pulling apart monsters in the WHL. This was the mid-1980s. Absolute beasts were on the ice in the Dub. Players like Stu Grimson, Todd Ewen, Shane Churla, Ken Baumgartner and Wendel Clark were throwing fists, trying to make a name for themselves on a nightly basis. Davis, a teenager, just like the players themselves, was right in the middle of it. "Wendel and Johnny Miner used to go to centre ice and fight, and they were best friends. They had just gotten done playing with Canada's national junior team together. It was one of the greatest fights ever."

Oh, and there were others. Future NHL heavies like Darin Kimble and Tony Twist, or was it Kelly Chase? "They threw and threw and threw. I just remember both of them putting their heads on their shoulders when we split them apart. I just looked at the other linesman. We were just seventeen, eighteen, nineteen years old ourselves, breaking it up."

Davis was eventually promoted from linesman to referee. He stuck with it and called games in the 1995 Memorial Cup. Before he knew it, refereeing was his life. "You talk to any of those old referees that made it to the NHL from the Western Hockey League and they will tell you that the Western League days were the greatest days of their lives—the stupidity and the fun and the responsibility and accountability for young guys. Sometimes, we were on the road for fourteen or fifteen days. We were twenty-four years old, living out of a suitcase, travelling around by airplane or in some linesman's car. Those were the Kerry Toporowski [505 minutes in penalties for Spokane in 1990–91] days, the Link Gaetz days, and with Bryan Maxwell screaming at you."

Maxwell coached in the Dub for the Spokane Chiefs during Davis's glory days in the league. Like a lot of guys in the league at the time, Davis sported a mullet. He had long, curly blond hair that looked quite similar to the locks donned by a more-than-popular wrestler at the time, Mr. Perfect. Maxwell, a hard-nosed player in his day, would give it to Davis from the bench: "'Davis, you think you're fucking perfect! You're fucking perfect! Look at you. You even look like Mr. Fucking Perfect.' Those days were great!"

And, like most of the players in the WHL, Davis dreamed of a pro career—in his case, as an official. His quest took him everywhere—all the way to the rough-and-tumble East Coast Hockey League. "I got sent to the East Coast League after being in the American League and the National League. I was kind of dejected. I was thinking, *What the hell?*"

The ECHL came with its share of adventure—and stories. "I got a great John Brophy story," Davis says of the legendary white-haired coach of the Hampton Roads Admirals. "I had him three games in a row. I had Brophy for my very, very first game ever in the East Coast League."

The game was in Toledo, Ohio. This was not the NHL. This was not the AHL. This was not the WHL. "The referees had to walk right through the lobby of the arena and up the stairs through the stands to get on the ice. Brophy had never seen me before. He didn't know me from Adam's cat. There was a pre-game ceremony before the game. The mayor of Toledo was coming out on the ice and Brophy was standing in the open gate on his team's bench. He was looking across the ice at me. He was trying to get the better of me before the game started. He was standing right in the open gate, in front of all of his players, with his arms crossed, looking straight at me. He wouldn't take his eyes off me."

This was classic John Brophy. He was trying to win the mind game before the hockey game even started. If Davis didn't want to stare down Brophy, he couldn't really find a lot of comfort when he looked behind Toledo's bench, either. Their head coach was Chris McSorley. That would be Marty's brother. Chris once had 545 penalty minutes (PIMs) in a single International League season. Davis's first ECHL game looked like it might be a baptism by fire. He didn't have to worry, though. Toledo came out flying. And Brophy only lasted for a period. "Brophy's team was down after the first. I think it was four or five zip. Their dressing room was across the way from our referees' room. Well, he starts walking directly at me. There was no reason for him to be upset at me. I said, 'Is everything okay, John?'"

Brophy was baffled. He looked back at Davis and belted out, "Is everything okay? Look at the fucking scoreboard! I'm going to watch *Home Improvement*!' That was his exact line. And Brophy never came out after that first period."

And that was it. Either John Brophy had had enough or he was just a huge Tim Allen fan. Brophy's assistant coach took over, and the Tool Time routine worked. "Brophy's team came back and won!"

Davis's days of wearing the stripes eventually came to an end. He took a couple of pucks to the head—literally. One night in Yorkton, Saskatchewan, while he was working one of the very few Tier II games on his sked, a defenceman went to clear the puck on a penalty kill. He ripped a slapshot. "I got to the top of the circle, which was pretty good for me. I turned back to watch the line changes and the puck caught me right on the side of the face. It almost took my eye out. I was a mess."

He wasn't only a mess. He was a tired, exhausted mess. A referee does not have any home games. It's one thing to constantly be on the road; it's another to constantly be on the road as the years go by. "I was probably in Seattle the night before and Yorkton, and the next day I might've been in Orlando, or Tallahassee the day after that, and

San Diego a couple days after that. I was just bouncing everywhere, it started to catch up."

The dream, at least Davis's dream of reaching the NHL wearing the stripes, was over. "It didn't look like it was going to happen at the NHL level. I was thinking, Yeah, *maybe I should get on with life.*

"There was still a three-man system for referees at the NHL level. The jobs were few and far between, and I had to make a decision. I was wandering around, driving in a linesman's car from Spokane to Portland, thinking, *This is the life,* for two hundred dollars and a thirty-dollar per diem. So, I kind of made up my mind that I was going to go home." He returned to Edmonton, where he now lived.

When he got home, Davis enrolled in a real estate course. But deep in his mind, he knew what he was supposed to do. "In my mind, I was always going to be a scout. I didn't know how I was going to do that, but I had grown up at Dad's kitchen table, which was Dad's scouting office. I knew the Gerry Melnyks and Leo Boivins that were having supper at our house every second night when they were on the road. And I was going to be that guy somehow, some way."

When he completed his real estate course, Davis opened a small office. He didn't stay there long. "I got a call from Kevin Prendergast, and then that very same day I got a call from Scott Bradley."

Prendergast was with the Oilers. Scott Bradley was with the Boston Bruins. When it rains, yes, it pours. The Oilers were looking for a scout; the Bruins were looking for a scout. Davis had a choice to make. He wanted the Boston gig. His dad, Lorne, was scouting with the Oilers. "I wanted that separation. I didn't want to be Lorne's little boy. I didn't need the nepotistic view of this."

The Bruins got back to Davis in a couple of weeks. They could only give him a part-time job. "I said, 'Let me see where I am at and I will get back to you.' At that point I phoned Kevin and he said, 'Well, do you want the job?'"

Davis was perplexed. The job was his if he wanted it. But he didn't want it that easily. "I don't have to interview for this? This is awkward enough," he told Prendergast.

"He said, 'Well, do you want to talk to Slats [Sather]?' I said, 'I've known Slats since I was twelve years old.' 'Well, do you want to talk to Bear [Barry Fraser, the team's scouting director]?' I said, 'I knew Bear before I knew Glen.' He said, 'Well, should *I* interview you?' I said, 'Man, who *don't* I know?' He said, 'How about Doug Risebrough?'"

That worked for Davis. He had never met Risebrough in his life. So, it was set—Davis would interview with Risebrough, the Oilers' vice-president of hockey operations. Davis was at a bar, watching a Cleveland Indians playoff game, when Risebrough called. He left the bar and met with Risebrough. He got the gig. But there was a catch: He had to move to Ontario. Davis was all in. He packed up a U-Haul and he and his now wife hit the road. They settled on the Kitchener-Waterloo area. Davis has lived there ever since.

The referee was now a scout. So, when he started, was he looking at the game as a referee or as a scout? Turns out there was not much difference. "There were a lot of similarities to it. It was wide focused and narrow focused. You have to narrow the herd in order to know what you're looking for, and to zoom in and get the information that you need to put people in priority, because truly that's what scouting is in this generation. It's prioritization. It's making a list. It's getting what you want or what you need. Watching the game as a scout was almost identical as it was to watching the game as a referee. You're trying to take in all of it and get the feel for all of it, and then I have to narrow in and watch this. It was very similar. I had probably always watched the game as a scout."

Those lessons from his dad were burned into Brad. "I don't ever remember cheering at a hockey game, maybe 2006 [when the Oilers made the Stanley Cup Final against Carolina]. Besides 2006, I don't know if I've ever cheered at a hockey game. When I was with my dad, he never cheered at a hockey game. Hockey was his job. He loved his job, but hockey was his job. We were never showing emotion. We were being in control of the situation. It was never an issue for me because we were sitting beside Dad and we had to watch how we handled ourselves. I think that I always watched the game as a scout."

Even though Davis had watched the game as a scout his entire life, there was still a lot to learn. His first draft with the Oilers was on June 28, 1998, in Buffalo, New York. Earlier that season, Davis had been enamoured with Michael Henrich of the Ontario Hockey League's Barrie Colts. Davis "fell in love" with the six-foot-two, 209-pound winger the first time he saw him. You never forget your first. "I fall in love with a lot of players. Who's the first? Michael Henrich. My very first year, and we took him in the first round."

Henrich had lit it up in his draft year for the Colts. He scored forty-one goals in sixty-six games. But Henrich never played a game in the NHL. He was the only player selected in the first round of the 1998 draft never to dress for an NHL game. It was a lesson learned for Davis. "A huge lesson, huge lesson for a first-year guy—putting his, for lack of a better term, balls on the table. Maybe I should say 'his name on the line.' But I was in my first year and I was stepping up for this guy. I always remember Nashville had the second pick that year. They took David Legwand. I remember talking to a few of the Nashville guys and they said it was between David Legwand and Michael Henrich."

If Nashville had taken Henrich with the second pick, Davis

wouldn't have learned his lesson. But he did—the hard way. "We took Henrich at fourteen, so other teams saw something that we didn't, but Nashville was on the same page as us."

Davis had learned—again, the hard way—the old mantra that you have to see a player at least six times. "For whatever reason, the very first time I ever saw Michael, I remember him having this just unbelievable game. He scored a couple of goals, he made a couple of hits, and whatever happened after that first time I saw him, I probably still had the goggles on from that first game. I wasn't good enough at the job yet to recognize that there was a whole year's worth of work that had to be put into this."

The 1998 draft wasn't a total bust for Davis and the Oilers, though. They got a kid with the ninety-ninth pick that Davis had scouted: Shawn Horcoff, a centre from Michigan State University who went on to play 1,008 NHL games. "To find him in the fourth round when we did, and we almost didn't sign Shawn because he couldn't skate! And then he became a great skater."

As a scout, you have to fight for who you believe in, but you also have to listen, sometimes even to your father. When Brad was scouting for the Oilers, Lorne was a member of the scouting staff as well. Their fights over players were legendary. "I loved working with my dad. We were getting in a car once and somebody said, 'Where are you guys going?' Kevin Prendergast was with us. He said, 'To watch the Davis boys fight again.'

"Dad and I used to go at it good. Really good, really good. Maybe my biggest lesson in scouting happened in a meeting where we were in Palm Desert, at Glen's place. There were, like, seven of us at the time there, maybe eight." A scout was at front of the room. He was the marker guy—this is pre-computer-tool days. The scout was writing down the names of all the players the Oilers were checking out.

After he wrote one name down, Brad and his dad started discussing the player. Before they knew it, father and son were in a full-on verbal war. "Dad's line was always the same. It was always 'Well, I know if I pick five of my guys, they'd kick the fucking shit out of all five of your fucking guys.' It was a stupid pissing match. It was a testosterone-laden, peacock-feathered battle. We were going at it, and going at it and going at it."

The screaming was at heavy metal levels. All of a sudden, though, the older Davis stopped screaming. "Dad said, 'Whoa. Hold on. That's a good point.' I got to tell you, I can't tell you a fucking thing that I said. Not one thing. I was fighting. I was trying to score points. I wasn't listening, but dad was listening. And that was my biggest scouting lesson: You are not there to win. You are there to help the staff. You're here to help the team. You're here to make the best selection.

"At times, I had my problems watching my emotions, and so did my dad. So, if your guy didn't go or your guy didn't get selected, or if you got told at the table that you should sit down and shut up—this isn't about you. That was the biggest lesson to me in all my years of scouting. It was when my dad, in the middle of a huge argument about a player, heard what somebody else said. And he stopped and said, 'Yeah. That's a good point.'

"He was somebody who had been around. He knew what he was doing. He knew what the bigger cause was. I didn't know that at the time."

That didn't, however, mean you don't go balls to the wall and scream and fight for your player. It just meant listen. It meant the team comes first. "There's been close to altercations in lots of scouting rooms. I think it was hard at the start not to take it personal. Barry Fraser and I went at it in one of my very first meetings. I had known Barry since my dad started in 1977 with Houston [of the WHA]. I went to Barry after to apologize to him, and that was the most shit I ever got in, was for apologizing. 'Don't you ever fucking apologize to me,' he said. 'If you think something, you fucking say it.' Barry gave me shit. He and I fought, and I apologized to him for fighting. He said, 'Don't ever apologize to me ever again for speaking your mind and saying what you want.'"

And sometimes, sticking up and fighting for a player that's a little off the radar can put you on an island.

The 2004–05 NHL season never happened. A labour dispute cancelled the season. Teams had no cash coming in, so they had to watch how they spent their pennies. That meant a scout like Brad Davis wouldn't be jetting off to Europe a few times that season on a scouting mission. He and the rest of the Oilers scouting staff would be sticking close to home. For Davis, that meant staying close to Kitchener-Waterloo. So, if you can't travel as much, and you have more time around home, why not broaden your horizons? Davis started to keep an eye on a kid who was playing Junior A in Toronto for the St. Michael's Buzzers. "Andrew Cogliano was a huge one for me. I am so proud that I found a nugget out of Junior A. We didn't do a whole lot of Junior A at the time."

Cogliano was a five-foot-ten, 180-pound centre. He was not going to destroy you physically. But he had something that drew Davis to him. Davis had been keeping an eye on Cogliano all throughout the regular season. His 102 points in forty-nine games were more than impressive. But it is what Cogliano did one night in the playoffs against the Wexford Raiders that convinced the Oilers scout that the Buzzers' young captain was the real deal. "Wexford had a young captain, too, named Nick Sucharski. [Sucharski was taken 136th overall by Columbus in the 2006 draft. He never played a game in the

NHL.] It was a war between St. Michael's and Wexford. Sucharski ended up making my list, too, because of this game. It was almost like Lecavalier and Iginla."

The year before Davis took in this St. Michael's–Wexford game, the Tampa Bay Lightning and Calgary Flames had met in the 2004 Stanley Cup Final. In Game Three, Flames superstar Jarome Iginla and his opposite number, Vincent Lecavalier, dropped the gloves. Two leaders making a statement on behalf of their respective teams. "Both coaches have got to be holding their breath," colour commentator Harry Neale said on the *Hockey Night in Canada* broadcast as the Calgary Saddledome crowd went wild. It was pure emotion. Davis was seeing the same thing a year later at a Junior A game when Cogliano and Sucharski fought.

"Those two met on the ice and just punched the shit out of each other. They just beat the piss out of each other. They were probably two of the youngest kids in the game. It was a great fight. Both of those guys were so good that playoff round. And when I saw Cogliano step up like that, I knew that passion was there. You talk about getting passionate on a guy, well, now I'm passionate on a guy."

Davis was sold on Cogliano. The 2005 draft was held at the Westin Hotel in Ottawa on July 30. It was somewhat of an unusual affair, scaled down because the NHL's labour stoppage had only come to an end eight days earlier, on July 22. Instead of massive tables on the floor of an NHL arena, teams had small desks on the floor of the Westin while the rest of their staffs would be huddled in rooms throughout the hotel. Not that Davis minded. "We had six guys on the floor. It was pretty early in Kevin Lowe's tenure as the GM. My dad and Stu MacGregor, who were the two Western scouts at the time, were at the table. The rest of us were up in this war room at the hotel with a line to the table. It was the best draft ever. We all had our suits and ties hanging in the closet in the hotel room and we were in our sweats. There was coffee, tea and all the food you could stuff in your face, and a bunch of guys in their gym shorts sitting around talking about the draft and watching it happen."

The first pick of the draft was the ultimate no-brainer. The Pittsburgh Penguins drafted Sidney Crosby with the first pick. All the Oilers and their casually dressed scouts could do was wait—Edmonton didn't pick until twenty-fifth. But the Oilers had a plan. They were going to take T. J. Oshie from Warroad High School in Minnesota with their pick. Lorne loved Oshie. Brad had his eye on Cogliano. But as Brad had learned, it was team first, and the Oilers had Oshie on their radar. There was just one problem for the Oilers, though: the St. Louis Blues.

Just a few months before the draft, Oshie finished off his final year of prep hockey in style. He led Warroad High to its first undefeated season, 29–0–2, in the school's sixty-three-year history. His team won the 2005 Minnesota State Class A championship. He led the entire state in scoring with one hundred points. But just as Brad Davis couldn't venture too far from home that season and ended up going head over heels for Andrew Cogliano, the St. Louis Blues had a scout who didn't have to travel too far from home, either. Mike Antonovich lived in Coleraine, Minnesota. He became the mayor of the small town in 2008 while still scouting for the Blues. Coleraine was three hours from Warroad. "Mike was an Iron Range [a rural mining area in Minnesota] guy and he is all over T. J. Oshie. He talked his staff and his people into T. J. Oshie being the guy."

The Blues selected Oshie with the twenty-fourth pick, one selection before the Oilers were set to take him. It was a great selection by the Blues: Oshie has played over a thousand NHL games. He is a Stanley Cup champion. But on that day in 2005 at the Westin, the Oilers did not have any time to ponder what a great selection St. Louis had just made. Oshie was gone. It was time to move on. And the Oilers only had a couple of precious minutes to make up their minds. They were on the clock. Lorne and Stu MacGregor were down at the table with Kevin Lowe because the Oilers had been expected to take Oshie. But he was gone. When the Blues took Oshie, the phone upstairs, where most of the Oilers staff was gathered, started ringing. "What do we do?" Davis begins. "And I pick up the phone and it is Kevin Lowe—my boss. I said we take Andrew Cogliano."

Kevin Lowe said, "Tell me about Andrew Cogliano." Davis gave his standard answer. "My line was always the same. 'He's Todd Marchant with hands.'"

Marchant was a former Oiler. He was a total speed demon who, in 2005, was still playing in the NHL for the Columbus Blue Jackets. "Not that Todd Marchant didn't have hands, but everybody accused him of that. If you could get another Todd Marchant with the twenty-fifth pick, you would have jumped at it. It wasn't meant to be a shot at Todd Marchant in any way. It was simply 'This is how much I like this guy. He can fly. He is competitive. He's everything.'

"It was probably on our list that way—that Andrew was the next guy, but we didn't have enough comparables of guys going back and forth and crossing over. Everybody didn't see Andrew Cogliano play. So, Kevin Lowe went with it, and what a soldier Andrew turned out to be."

After two seasons at the University of Michigan, Cogliano made the Oilers out of his first pro camp in 2007. He played in all eighty-two regular-season games for the Oilers that year. He once played in 830 consecutive NHL games, good enough for eighth on the all-time list. He won a Stanley Cup with the Colorado Avalanche in the spring of 2022. He retired after the 2023–24 season. His final stat line: 190 goals, 274 assists and 464 points in 1,294 regular-season games. He was with the Oilers for his first four NHL seasons before he was traded to Anaheim on July 12, 2011, for a second-round pick. "I remember when they traded Cogliano. It was 'Well, he won't accept anything but being a top-line guy.' That's what I was told. Well, he is still playing," Davis said at the time of this interview. "And he has shown his character of doing whatever you asked him to do. Andrew Cogliano, bless his heart."

The next year, at the 2006 draft, Brad Davis and the Oilers had to play the waiting game again. This time, they didn't pick until number forty-five. If you can find a future NHLer at forty-five, you're doing a more than solid job. The Oilers had their work cut out for them. The team had gone on an incredible run to the 2006 Stanley Cup Final against Carolina, losing in seven games. Remember, 2006 was one of the few times David had ever cheered at a hockey game. Now it was back to business, although a lot of the business took place right in the middle of the party. "Our meetings suffered because we were in the Stanley Cup Final. I remember meeting in the wives' lounge during the day. [The scouts] were all in for the finals against Carolina."

The Oilers brass had to balance the final series and their draft prep. And at the same time, Brad Davis had to let the team know about the latest player to steal his heart that season. "I fell in love with Jeff Petry, and everybody else kind of liked Jeff Petry, but I loved Jeff Petry."

Petry was a six-foot-three, 209-pound defenceman from Ann Arbor, Michigan, who was playing junior for the Des Moines Buccaneers in the USHL. He was committed to Michigan State University. He was a long way from NHL-ready, but hey, that's what scouts have to do, project what a kid will be like two or even five years down the road. "I thought there was so much upside to him, but we didn't pick until forty-five. We had no first-rounder. Kevin Prendergast, who was my boss, was running the meeting. He finally said, 'I've had enough! Where the fuck do you want Petry!' because I kept bringing him up and bringing him up and bringing him up. Nobody else was on it, and I wouldn't shut up. There is a time to back off and there is a time you've gotta stand up and go with what you truly feel. And everybody else loved him, just not as much as I did. But I had seen him the most."

Davis was fighting for his guy. He believed in this Petry kid. He turned out to be right. But there were times he turned out to be wrong as well. It is in those meetings where a scout can truly shine or . . . not shine. "There are probably three people in the world who can tell the rest of the world how good a scout is. There is the chief scout, the guy who reads the reports, and a couple other scouts in the room. They know the democratic process—or non-democratic process [of a pre-draft chat]—that plays out in that room. I lost a lot of battles on guys that were good. There were a lot of players that I wish that the other guys in the room would've listened to me on. But fuck, I got a silo full of guys that I don't want anybody to know about. I don't want anyone to know where I had them on my list, too!"

But Davis was bang on when it came to Petry. "I think I had Petry on our list at around twelve or fourteen."

So, Edmonton waited. When the forty-fifth pick in the 2006 NHL Entry Draft came up, the first by the Oilers, Petry was still there. They got him. Then Davis's flip phone stared buzzing. Davis lives in the same city as a scout named Joe McDonnell, who was the director of amateur scouting for Detroit at the time. The Red Wings had the next pick. McDonnell sent Davis a text on the flip phone—Davis was rather new to the texting game in 2006. "I barely knew what to do. The texting was so new . . . All it said was 'fuck you.' Maybe he wanted Petry," Davis laughs. "We've never talked about it, but that was the message I got on my phone."

Jeff Petry is currently at more than 970 regular-season NHL games, and counting. He has played the second-most games of any defenceman selected in the 2006 draft, trailing only the first-overall pick, Erik Johnson.

Brad Davis's last year with the Edmonton Oilers, and in the NHL, was the 2013–14 season. It was a no-brainer year for the Oilers. Once they won the draft lottery, everyone on the planet knew the Oilers were going to take Connor McDavid with the first-overall pick. Davis still remembers the first time he saw McDavid, when he was playing junior in Erie, Pennsylvania. "The arena was for indoor football or whatever else they played there, so it was tough to get a good sight line. Even though we had great seats, there was nobody in the building."

Davis did what most scouts do, going up to a high corner of the rink. It didn't take him long to see what everyone else was seeing, what the hockey world was raving about. "Ten minutes into the game. I was lifted off my seat. I told you I never watched games emotionally in my life as a scout, but I remember being physically lifted off of my seat from emotion, from what I saw. And this boy was fifteen years old! I was thinking that I'm in Erie, Pennsylvania, and I wish that I had sat in a place where I could tell people how good this kid was!"

By the time the Oilers selected Connor McDavid with the first pick in June 2015, Davis's NHL scouting days were over. He was let go by the Oilers just before the draft. "I remember when I lost my job . . . I did the meetings and everything. I had the shakes. I was in a panic. How is my life going to change? I was used to getting up at four in the morning, getting in the car, getting to Pearson [airport] if my flight was at eight or ten or noon so I didn't have to fight traffic because I was so comfortable with all my 'status.' And if I had a flight cancelled, well, I didn't have to worry about it because a concierge would come and take care of me because of my status, and then I would go check in at the Marriott and they would say, 'Oh we've got the best suite for you.'"

Status for Brad Davis meant that he was a high-flying, hotel-staying NHL scout. But that was gone. He had to adjust. He was no longer Brad Davis of the Edmonton Oilers. He was now just Brad Davis. "I was on my rowing machine downstairs when I finally started to get my head around it. You always tell kids not to let things like the draft define you. You have to bring yourself back down afterwards and be a normal person."

Davis is still in hockey. He works with Prospect 285 in the Kitchener-Waterloo area, mentoring and advising young hockey players. The lessons he learned from a life in hockey, that started at his dad's kitchen table, are being passed on. "I have never been happier in my entire life, except for those Western Hockey League days as a referee. I'm helping kids that so want to learn. I have information, stories and that education from my dad to pass along. Dad's voice is in my head every day. I'm of way more value in the game giving back to it than I was taking from it, which is what scouting was."

CHAPTER 3

Canadian Content

James Boyd

James Boyd (right) celebrates a World Junior Championship in Halifax, Nova Scotia, with 67's and Hockey Canada strength and conditioning coach Sean Young and 67's and Team Canada defenceman Jack Matier. COURTESY JAMES BOYD

Toronto's Ted Reeve Arena is like a lot of other small rinks around Toronto. It has a decent canteen, and trophy cases line a few of the walls. But it is perhaps best known—at least to some cinema connoisseurs—as the home of the fictional Hamilton Mustangs. That's the team Rob Lowe's character played for in the 1986 hockey film *Youngblood*. The on-ice scenes for the film were shot at the arena. Unlike a lot of other rinks that boast that an NHLer suited up there once upon a time, if you ask around Ted Reeve, someone may mention that Rob Lowe and Patrick Swayze once dazzled—at least fictionally—right here.

Still, despite its Hollywood pedigree, Ted Reeve is a long way away from the star-studded world of big-league hockey. It is not home to a Junior A team, and it is not home to any of the teams in Toronto's highly competitive Greater Toronto Hockey League AAA loop, a league that has produced, among others, Connor McDavid and Steven Stamkos. It is, however—on one February night, at least—where you will find Ottawa 67's general manager James Boyd taking in a high school hockey game. "There are lots of AAA players playing high school hockey. This is one of the best places to find a hidden gem."

Maybe when you were in high school, you crammed for the odd test or exam. A year and a half before he was watching this high school hockey game at Ted Reeve Arena, Boyd was cramming for the ultimate hockey test: leading Canada's management group into the 2022 World Junior Hockey Championship. There was just one problem. The tournament was delayed. Now, if you were in high school and a test was delayed, that would be a dream come true. That was not the case for Boyd, Team Canada's general manager, and the rest of his staff. COVID delayed the 2022 World Juniors from its traditional Christmas-to-New-Year's slot on the hockey calendar to August. A lot can happen in eight months in junior hockey. Players Boyd had on his team eight months earlier were a no-go for the summer tournament. "Heading into that tournament, there was a lot of uncertainly with player availability. It actually was a pretty hectic timeframe."

Boyd had done his homework and had already assembled a Team Canada roster eight months earlier, at the tournament's traditional time. On December 29, 2021, after a third game had to be cancelled due to a positive COVID test, the International Ice Hockey Federation decided to cancel the tournament. It was eventually rescheduled for August. Sounds good for the players on that December team, but in reality, it was anything but. A who's who of players—guys such as Cole Perfetti, Owen Power, Jake Neighbours—were not made available for the August makeup date. That meant it was back to the drawing board for Boyd and his staff.

"Some of the guys we couldn't take were pretty obvious—like Jamie Drysdale," said Boyd. "He's a regular in the NHL. There were a number of players who played for us in December at the cancelled tournament who weren't available anymore in the summertime."

The number stood at seventeen. That means seventeen players had to be immediately scratched off Team Canada's list. But somehow Boyd and Team Canada found their way into the tournament final against Finland on August 20. The game went into overtime tied 2–2. Kent Johnson, a forward from the University of Michigan, scored the winner for Canada. But that's not the moment most Canadian hockey fans remember.

A little over a minute before Johnson won it for Canada, Mason McTavish saved it for Canada when he miraculously stopped a puck from going into the Canadian net in overtime. The puck was dangling over the goal line—in mid-air, on its way home—when, with the hand-eye coordination of Ty Cobb, McTavish swatted it out of the air. It would have been a silver medal for Canada; instead, it was gold. And that meant it was gold for James Boyd, who, along with his staff, had crammed like hell to put together a Team Canada for the second time in a year.

"Scouting is the key. I worked hand in hand with Alan Millar at that time. He is now in Regina with the Pats, and at that time he was full time with Hockey Canada. We really split the responsibilities of getting out Canada-wide and watching the players."

Incredibly enough, less than five months later, Boyd and Canada won gold again. This time, the players and staff weren't sequestered in a hotel, as they had been in Edmonton. They were as much a part of the tournament and the madness in Halifax as they could be. But in many ways, it was hockey déjà vu. Canada, with Boyd once again serving as the team's GM, reached the final. The team Boyd and his staff had assembled kept pace with the Czech Republic, and after sixty minutes, the game was tied, 2–2—again. Overtime was about to begin. Scotiabank Centre was packed. The city, and the entire country, were ready to erupt. Boyd was with the rest of the Team Canada brass in their suite above the ice. He knew the routine, he knew the feeling.

"When you get those games and you're in the management part, the feeling is really helpless. I go back to when I was coaching. You can influence the game, you're involved, you're making lineup changes, you're invested in the game. I'm up there just chewing my nails and hoping for the best."

"The best" happened after six minutes and twenty-two seconds of pure stress. Team Canada forward Dylan Guenther broke into the Czech zone on a two-on-one with Joshua Roy. Guenther, born and bred in Edmonton, Alberta, and a defenceman for his hometown Edmonton Oil Kings of the Western Hockey League, made a quick pass to Joshua Roy on the left wing. Roy, from Saint-Georges de Beauce, Quebec, and who skated for the Sherbrooke Phoenix in what was then called the Quebec Major Junior Hockey League, held on to the puck just long enough for the Czech defenceman to fall and make a wild stab at the puck. Roy waited just a second before making his pass across the ice to Guenther. A quick shot by Guenther, and the tournament was over. James Boyd and the Team Canada brass, who had scouted and assembled these players from all over Canadian junior and American college hockey, roared. It was gold for Canada again. "I was so happy for the players and the staff. It was a moment of recognition, of all the work that goes into it—the coaches, all the scouting network, everyone."

When you put together back-to-back Team Canadas, you are relying on several things. To start with, you need to see the results from the scouting that had already been done for Canada's under-17 and under-18 programs. But you are also depending on yourself, on your own eyeballs. "It's easy to get the list of players you're evaluating as part of that team," said Boyd. "You're having discussions with the coaching staff—how do they want to play? You're involving the coaching staff in deciding on the pool of players. And then the deeper assessment—that's the fun part of it. Alan Millar and I became very good friends over the process. We talked every day. I'd be up in Owen Sound, and he'd say, 'I was just in Lethbridge.'"

Putting together the players for Team Canada also offered a change in philosophy for Boyd, as opposed to how he put together his Ottawa 67's club.

"When putting together the 67's, a big part of that is projections. You're thinking three months, six months, four years down the road.

Whereas the World Juniors is right now. The World Juniors has a really important component of team-building. It's not an All-Star team. You're building a team to be able to compete in the tournament. We always say that the World Juniors is not a place to get your game back or rekindle your confidence. You need the best players at that time."

Boyd hit the road. He got in his vehicle and drove. He headed east, throughout Quebec and farther east, watching as many kids who were on his radar as he could. Boyd would watch games on his way east, and then he would watch games on his way back home as well.

One of the players he wanted to check out was Joshua Roy. Boyd was looking for players who could fill certain roles on his team. He had scorers, but he was also looking for someone who could kill penalties. He thought Roy might be able to do that. The problem was that Roy was not on the penalty kill for his Sherbrooke Phoenix team. What did Boyd do?

"Steve Julien was Joshua's coach in Sherbrooke. He sang Roy's praises as an intelligent player who is very adaptable."

More often than not, when a player makes a national team, he has to take on a role that he does not perform with his club team. In Roy's case, it was the PK. "Josh ended up being our best penalty killer at the world juniors. It's getting that information and talking to coaches. It is doing a lot of that investigative work behind the scenes and taking that information and trying to build the best team. Scouting for a short-term tournament is intense, very much so."

Roy was on the team that won gold in Edmonton and was on the team that won gold in Halifax, making him one of eight players who played in both tournaments for Canada. Having players like Connor Bedard, Logan Stankoven and Brennan Othmann play in both tournaments was a luxury for Team Canada and its scouting staff. Off the ice, a number of the staff took part in both tournaments as well. "I think it's really important for continuity. The fact that we had Dennis Williams, the head coach [in Halifax], on our staff in the summertime [Williams was an assistant coach in Edmonton]. A number of the staff had returned and were familiar with the process. So [the returning players and staff] gained a lot of experience in a short period of time."

A short time is what Boyd had to put together the rest of his team for the 2023 tournament in Halifax. The gold medal game in Edmonton was on August 20, leaving Boyd and his staff about three months to get their team in order for Halifax. So, there was not a ton of time to soak it all in. "It was a short break, and then right into our CHL [Canadian Hockey League] team's training camp. By early September, I was in Traverse City, Michigan, watching the NHL rookie camp there. I was already right back at it, so there wasn't much transition."

Boyd would scout, Alan Millar and others would scout, and then they would report back to each other and the Team Canada coaching staff. "To a certain extent, you're eliminating players," says Boyd. He was looking for players who would match up against the opposition at the tournament and players who could adapt, like Joshua Roy, if they had to. "What if the guys you're looking at are all centres? You're trying to determine if they can fill a specific role on the team."

It was a lot of work, a lot of hockey games to watch, a lot of names to eliminate in a short amount of time. "I think you have to take the history of a player into account a little bit," said Boyd. There is really valuable info on most of the players from the under-17 and under-18 programs—not just from the tournament itself, but the evaluations. Hockey Canada provides the scouting that goes into the selection for those tournaments to you. You're evaluating a player who might be in a different situation. You have players that are playing on juggernaut teams, and you have players that are playing on teams that are struggling to make the playoffs. That's just the way it goes. You're trying to catch the games that are going to be competitive games. You're looking at the schedule [choosing the games you want to watch]. That is a really key part of evaluating the players as well. What games are you going to be able to catch? You hope that they're good games. You hope the games you go to see are not going to be blowouts. But the clock is ticking. The hourglass gets turned over, and the tournament comes quick. Training camps start at the end of August, and then you're picking the team the last week of November. You have to send the names of your players in to the IIHF the last week of November. It is a lot of work in a short amount of time."

As Boyd told me earlier, when you are scouting to put together a Team Canada, you are not putting together an All-Star team. You are looking for players who can score, kill penalties, play defence. You are looking for players who can handle the physical grind as your team gets deeper into the tournament. Above all, you need depth. You need players who can step up if an opportunity presents itself.

For example? Jack Matier is a big (six-foot, four-inch, 205-pound) defenceman from Sault Ste. Marie, Ontario. Boyd did not have to go far to see him play: Jack played on Boyd's Ottawa 67's. He's not a first-rounder; he was drafted 124th overall by Nashville in 2021, but he's not short on talent, either. Boyd liked what he saw in Matier for his team in Halifax.

"He had a positive experience on the under-18 team when he won a gold medal. He was also one of the top-scoring defencemen in the OHL leading up to the tournament. The advantage for Jack was that he played for Dave Cameron and me in Ottawa. When it gets down to compiling your team, the question sometimes comes down to 'If there's an injury or a suspension, who is a good penally killer?' 'Who could play on the power play in a pinch?' We had all these different questions. We had inside knowledge on Jack. We knew he could do all of those things." Matier played in seven tournament games. He put up one assist and finished a plus-4.

Matier spent most of his first professional season, 2023–24, with the Atlanta Gladiators, the ECHL affiliate of the Nashville Predators. "Jack started in the ECHL because I think Nashville has done a heckuva job drafting defencemen. On their American Hockey League team, they have a depth of defencemen, so that's the situation for Jack this year. I know he's really taking it seriously, becoming a pro in his first year. I really think he's going find his way to the NHL because of his character and the type of competitor he is. Everyone has a different journey."

Then there is the easy work, if there is such a thing. When a player from the pros gets sent down, you do have to eliminate a name from the bottom, but you're getting a quality player on the top. Take Shane Wright. A once-upon-a-time projected first-overall pick in the NHL draft, he went fourth overall to Seattle in 2022. Wright started the fall of 2022 in the NHL, then he was assigned to the AHL. Wright eventually was made available to Boyd and Team Canada. Boyd didn't have any worries about Wright. "It was a no-brainer to put him on the team based on his past experience. Do you want to talk about character? You want to talk about performance in the previous tournaments? It was all there. He bumped around a little bit [that fall]. He was probably looking forward to the experience."

Wright had seven points in seven tournament games and was a crucial part of the team. So was Connor Bedard. The then-seventeen-year-old phenom had an incredible twenty-three points in seven games. He was named tournament MVP. You might ask if, with a phenom like Bedard, you are scouting for players you think will fit in alongside him, play on a line with him. "No, we don't. We leave that to the coaches. They probably have an idea of the lines. We talk in the off-season and leading up to the tournament about what the line combinations might be, and who's going to play with who. It never ends up being that way, though."

The challenge with a kid like Bedard, if there was one, was to make sure his off-ice demands didn't become a burden to his on-ice ones. That problem didn't fall under Boyd's scouting role; he had to deal with it when wearing his general manager hat. "There are two parts to it. Part one: There are a lot of media requirements for a player like him, and there should be. He's a superstar. As the tournament goes along, you try to support him as much as you can with all of the other responsibilities. You try to make sure that he is getting enough downtime and that sort of thing. We know the interviews need to happen and people want to hear about Connor Bedard. I get it. But we also need him to play, making sure he has the tools to do the job. That's the nutrition and that sort of thing. That goes for all of our players. Part two: When the tournament starts, you go to support mode. You need to make sure, to the best of our ability, that when the players arrive at the rink, their mind is clear and they are going to enjoy playing a hockey game and not have to worry about all the other stuff."

If it all works out, like it did for Boyd, you win gold—twice. Both times in overtime, in a span of five months—first in the bubble in Edmonton and then in Halifax. "I was elated—elated by the experience in the summertime in Edmonton. It was a different experience because of the COVID cancellation, and all that was really a journey. We were in isolation. As a team, we were sequestered in a hotel. You were in your own room for days at a time. Halifax was the opposite.

It was pandemonium in the city as soon as Dylan scored. It was like the roof blew off."

There is also relief. When you're the GM of Team Canada and you lose, the second-guessing begins. When you're Canada and you win, there is, among all those other feelings, relief. The players you put together won. "When you're talking about the World Juniors, there is definitely a feeling of relief. I believe that Canada has success because we have to win. That was real. That was very real. It was a different type of pressure."

And if you're Canada and you win, there isn't a ton of pressure, but incredibly, there can still be second-guessing—from the fans, from the media, even from the brass.

"As a manager, and as a scout, there were decisions that in retrospect could've worked out differently. We did not take Wyatt Johnston to Edmonton. At the time we made the decision on who we were bringing to camp, he was playing well, and he was in the discussion. But we thought he was right on the line. We thought he would be ready next year. And then he just exploded. Wyatt became the best player in the league, and then the following year he played in the National Hockey League and people were saying—ourselves included—'Why didn't I see that? Why didn't we see that? What happened? Wyatt exploded! What if we brought him to the tournament? How would it have been different?' There are so many good players in the CHL and US and Canadian college hockey. There will be second-guessing. I guess if you don't win, you could put together different versions of the team forever. Forever," he repeats.

And Boyd has been around the game literally forever. Believe me, he knows what he's talking about. He broke into the OHL with the Kitchener Rangers as a seventeen-year-old. The next season, he was traded to the Ottawa 67's. He billeted with the team's legendary coach and GM, Brian Kilrea.

"I lived with Brian and Judy Kilrea," said Boyd. "Killer was very much a grandfather figure. Judy would make fresh bread every day. There were a couple of players living there down in the basement. We'd watch hockey with Killer at night. Killer would sit in his chair. He had one of those ashtrays that's actually a tractor tire, and he would smoke cigars and watch hockey."

After a couple more years in the OHL, Boyd enrolled at the University of Guelph. But by the 1999–2000 season he was back in the OHL as a twenty-three-year-old assistant coach with the Belleville Bulls. "Up until that point in my life, I had never considered coaching. My plan was 'I will do it for a year, and then go to grad school.'"

Boyd never did go to grad school, though he did finish his history degree at the University of Guelph. He hasn't left the OHL, either. Boyd is still looking to win that elusive OHL championship with Ottawa. But he did make junior hockey history with Team Canada, winning an incredible two World Juniors in a span of just 140 days. "I had incredible people around me—the program of excellence management group, guys like Alan I mentioned before, and [Hockey Canada senior vice-president] Scott Salmond, and the rest of the people, the support staff and the coaches. The amount of time and energy we spent was enormous. Preparing those teams for that tournament, in the middle of a really unique time, in the middle of a pandemic, was a challenge; we weren't even really sure what the rules and regulations were going to be from province to province. We had kids in Ontario who didn't play hockey the year before. It was unique and it required a lot of thinking on the fly . . . actually, a lot of reacting on the fly. It was a really collaborative effort. It was really intense when the whole thing was over. You just take a deep breath and say, 'Oh, my goodness, what an experience that was.'"

What do you do when it's over? If you're James Boyd, you go back to doing what you love: You go back to the rink. You keep watching hockey. Because you love it. Because you have more work to do. Because you want to bring an OHL championship to Ottawa. That's why you can find the man who helped make Canadian hockey history at a small rink in the east end of Toronto, watching a high school game. It's the type of game many fans or even scouts wouldn't bother with. But Boyd lives for this.

"I love watching hockey. I try to get out whenever I'm able. I try to watch as much hockey as I can. You never know what you're going to see. There are players who have come into the OHL out of the blue from lower-level hockey, not AAA hockey. There are always different circumstances of why players could be playing at a lower level. Maybe they are a multi-sport athlete. Maybe their parents are recently divorced. Maybe there is some extenuating circumstance. If there is a game and I'm able to go, it's fun to go watch."

CHAPTER 4

Planting the Scouting Seed

Ken Fox

Ken Fox was the head scout of the Kamloops Blazers when they selected current NHL star Logan Stankoven fifth overall for the Blazers in the 2018 WHL Bantam Draft. COURTESY KEN FOX

Depending on what kind of hockey fan you are, you can look at the game and the search for the next great player in any number of ways. Maybe you like the numbers side of the game. You can look at the fancy stats to try and nail down the next great player. Or maybe you're more of a meat-and-potatoes kind of fan—you want to get a look at a player and see if he has the basic building blocks of what it may take. Or maybe you look at the search for the next great player as some sort of quest. Maybe you envision a scout combing the Prairies, going from town to town during an endless Western Canadian winter. That's a nice, romantic look at what scouting is. In reality, though, it is a little less romantic.

WHL scout Ken Fox and fellow Red Deer Rebels scout Carter Sears set out one winter day on a four-and-a-half-hour drive to scout a little-known bantam player in Russell, Manitoba. Their main priority on the drive from Holdfast, Saskatchewan, to Russell was not to turn into icicles.

"Carter had an old [Ford] Tempo and the heater barely worked. We had to put a blanket beside the door on the passenger side to make sure we didn't freeze to death. It was a lot different back then than it is now," says Fox, now retired.

Fox spends part of his winters these days in a much warmer place, Phoenix, Arizona. The 2022–23 hockey season was his first as a retired scout. For the previous thirty-plus years, he spent his winters around Western Canada, scouting first for the Red Deer Rebels, then the Vancouver Giants, Swift Current Broncos and finally the Kamloops Blazers. His scouting adventure began simply enough: He answered a classified ad. Fox had played at Notre Dame College in Wilcox, Saskatchewan, as a teen. After that, he hit the Saskatchewan senior hockey circuit, playing for the Imperial Sabres. Once he hung up the blades, though, the Saskatchewan grain farmer needed to get his hockey fix somehow. His summers were more than busy tending to his six thousand acres, but now, with no games to play, he needed to occupy his time in those cold prairie winters somehow. A classified ad the Red Deer Rebels had placed in *The Hockey News* was his answer. The Rebels were looking for a scout in southern Saskatchewan. That seemed like just the right fit for the Holdfast farmer.

"I still live in Holdfast, about an hour north of Regina, sort of in between Saskatoon and Regina. That's sort of how I got into it. I was about an hour from Regina, about forty-five from Moose Jaw, and about an hour and a half from Saskatoon. I was pretty central to Saskatchewan, so it worked out pretty well."

It worked out very well for Fox. He got the gig with the Rebels. And that's how he found himself in a beat-up Ford Tempo, barrelling across the prairie to check out future NHLer Aaron Asham in Russell, Manitoba.

"It was a lot different back then than it is now. Now, you tend to fly a little more and you're more into major cities than going to the one-horse towns. We used to put a lot more kilometres on our cars because we were going everywhere."

In the early 1990s, you had to go to where the players were. There were no live streams of games that you could watch a kid on. No one had highlight videos posted to the internet. A Rebels bird dog in southern Manitoba had put the word out to Fox and the team that they should check out a kid named Aaron Asham. He was playing against some pretty weak competition, but Fox and Sears decided to jump into that Tempo and make the drive anyway.

"Back then, it was word of mouth, and then you would have to go watch him. Aaron was not playing at a great level. He was so much better than anybody else, and you knew he was going to be that much better once he got to the next level," says Fox. "Back in those days, you were able to find guys like that a little more than you can nowadays. In a sense, you could hide guys back then a little bit more."

A few years after Fox first saw him, Asham was one of the top point producers on the Red Deer Rebels. In his third year on the team, he had forty-five goals and ninety-six points. In his final year with the Rebels, his fourth in the WHL, he scored forty-three goals and ninety-two points. He also played with an edge. He never had fewer than 126 penalty minutes in a season during his WHL days. He was a third-round pick of the Montreal Canadiens in 1996 who went on to play in 789 regular-season games in the NHL. So, what did Fox see early on?

"Aaron was very passionate. He wanted to win. At times it maybe got him in a little trouble, but he wanted to win, to win at all costs."

But Fox didn't just watch Asham on the ice. He met his parents as well, trying to figure out what kind of kid he was dealing with, and maybe, let's be honest, just how big Aaron would become.

"I met his dad and mom. You could tell that they were passionate, too. You knew that he was going to want to get better and play a better level of hockey. Back in those days, sometimes it was hard to get a player to leave those small towns to play in a better hockey environment. That was very important back in the early days."

Asham was one of the first players Fox could look at and say, "Yeah, I know what I'm doing." Despite that, though, the moustached Sasky grain farmer learned on the job.

"The first time I went out was with Carter. He was the head scout at the time. He can be a little bit intimidating. He's quite a character. He's lots of fun to be around. I was nervous. You think, *Oh yeah, I know what a hockey player is, I think this guy can play, I should list this guy,* and that kind of stuff. But you find out pretty quickly that there's a lot more to it than knowing sort of what you think a hockey player is. You have to do some homework. You have to do some digging.

"There are a lot of things I look for," Fox continued. "Character, for me, was very important. You always talk to coaches. I was one of those guys who liked to talk to schoolteachers about the kids. What they were like with their classmates? What they were like in school? I wanted to know what their work ethic was like on and off the ice. I found that was very important."

Character is the word Ken Fox uses to describe a player the Red Deer Rebels took in the sixth round of the 1996 WHL Bantam Draft. When I mention the name Colby Armstrong, the first thing Fox does is laugh. "When I hear the name Colby Armstrong, I think character. *A* character."

Fox knew Colby's dad, Wayne, and his mother, Rosemary. Wayne was a former senior hockey player and Rosemary was a figure skater. So, he knew Colby had pedigree. But when he was scouting him in midget, the Armstrong kid was just skin and bones. Still, he was scoring and playing with the kind of edge that perhaps would be better suited to the next level, the WHL.

"I wouldn't say he didn't get in trouble a few times, whether it was with the coaches or his teammates. He was another guy that was very passionate. He worked hard. He was always living on the edge. He wasn't afraid to say what he thought—sometimes to coaches. Coaches really liked him, but there was the odd coach that didn't like him because he was pretty vocal about what he thought, but he worked hard, and he expected the same from everybody else. So, every once in a while, that would get him in trouble. If somebody was slacking off a little bit and wasn't working as hard . . ." Fox laughs.

"The thing with Colby," Fox continues, "is he was a buck fifty, and that is stretching it probably, but he wasn't afraid of anything. He was physical. It didn't matter what the size of the other guy was, he never backed down from anybody."

Fox saw in Colby Armstrong a passionate, skinny kid with good pedigree who had a brass set of balls. But would it work at the major junior level?

"I remember when he came to Red Deer. He was playing AAA midget in Saskatchewan. It wasn't going great. But finally, they brought him into Red Deer, and it was a good move for him because he wasn't afraid to play at that next level, even at his size. I think he wanted it so bad that he would do anything, whatever the coach wanted him to do."

There were things that Colby could do at the WHL level that he simply could not do at the Midget AAA level. Playing at that higher level suited his style better. "If the coach wanted him to go run a guy over, or get in the corner, or drive the net, Colby would do it. Whereas in AAA midget, sometimes you can't play that kind of way. But at the major junior level, you can. And I think that's made him into the player that he was and where he ended up."

"I would see Ken all over the place," said Armstrong. "He's this tiny little guy who is great to talk to, and I had extra time with him. I knew him through my dad, who did some scouting as well, so I got to know him a little bit better. He is the initial pipeline guy of getting a lot of kids' careers started and having a book on them and scouting them. It does mean something for me that he kind of got me started. A guy like Ken really takes an interest in you. You got to imagine that they push to draft you. They put you in their scouting reports all that time. Red Deer drafted me in the sixth round. It wasn't like I was high up on anybody's list. They took a shot on me. I ended up playing there. We won a Memorial Cup. And shortly after that, I became a first-round NHL pick. Time kind of flew by. In some way or another,

I made those guys look like geniuses for picking me that late," Armstrong laughs.

The 2001 Memorial Cup champion Red Deer Rebels were a team that Fox played a huge part in building by helping to draft and sign players. "Some players worked out, and there's no doubt over the years that some players didn't. But there's lots that did."

After that Memorial Cup win, it was time for Ken Fox to move on. He joined the Vancouver Giants for the next five years, where he served as a scout. Then it was a quick one-year stop in Swift Current, Saskatchewan, for the 2007–08 season, where he was assistant director of scouting. The next year, he was back with the Giants as their head scout. Then, after one year in Vancouver, he joined the Kamloops Blazers as their head scout. The guy who answered that ad in the *The Hockey News* was now a grizzled WHL veteran. "They called me 'head scout,' but basically I was just scouting everywhere."

The game was changing. Back in Fox's early days of scouting, he had to deal with parents who were perhaps reluctant to send their kids to a far-off town to pursue their hockey dreams. He would have to earn the trust of the parents. Now he had to earn the trust of the parents *and* deal with player agents. "Nothing against agents, but when I first started scouting, you would never see agents until the players were eighteen years old. Not like now. You see agents when the players are fourteen, fifteen, sixteen years old. So, you're dealing more with agents nowadays, but back then you were dealing with the parents. You still deal with the parents now, but it's not quite the same as it was back then."

And now—and in Fox's later years in the game—you could scout a player without racking up the mileage on a decrepit Ford Tempo. Games are streamed online now, there are online scouting services, and those small towns where you could maybe hide a player? Well, everyone knows about them, and you don't have to go to them as much, either. "It is a lot easier now, no doubt about it, as opposed to when I first started. Now the major tournaments are in all the major cities. There's no doubt you spend way more time in Brandon and Winnipeg, those kinds of places."

The circumstances around how you see a player may have changed, but scouting that player, for the most part, remained the same for Ken Fox. You have to see the player. Maybe it's not in a one-horse town anymore, but you still need to know what you are looking at. You still need to see the potential.

Fox took a kid out of Saskatoon for the Blazers with a second-round pick in the 2016 bantam draft. Connor Zary reminded him of Colby Armstrong. Fox, despite the changing times, was still the same scout he always was. "I think I stayed the same. Connor Zary, in a way, isn't a lot different from Colby Armstrong. We ended up getting him in the second round, which was a steal at the time in the bantam draft. He was passionate. Sometimes, he'd get on his teammates if they weren't working hard enough. And that's how we lucked out a little bit in getting him in the second round. It worked out well for Kamloops, and it worked out well for him because he is very passionate."

That passion has taken Zary all the way to the NHL with the Calgary Flames. "Connor's the same. I wouldn't call Connor a great skater, an elite skater, but he is not afraid of anything. He is smart and he will drive the net hard. That's why he scores goals, because he is not afraid to go to the net."

Fox watches the NHL as a retired scout. In that first winter away from the game, he still found himself in the rink. He has a grandson who was playing Midget AAA in Swift Current. "I went to the Mac's tournament in Calgary. I saw everyone around again. I've been to a few WHL games and quite a few AAA midget games, watching my grandson, and you see the other guys [the scouts] and right away you start thinking, *I do miss it.* But I spent lots of winters away and my wife and I, we came down here to Phoenix for a month. We're renting a place. I'm playing a little pickleball, a little golf. It's okay," he chuckles.

Even in Phoenix, though, Ken's wife, Jessica, can't keep him out of the rink. Before the Arizona Coyotes relocated to Utah, he was at a game, checking out one of his old players, Connor Ingram, who was playing goal for the Coyotes against the Pittsburgh Penguins. Once upon a time, Ingram was just a raw kid playing minor hockey in Saskatchewan.

"I listed Connor with Kamloops. He was a bit of a free spirit. He wasn't even a draft pick."

Fox and the Blazers had to meet with Ingram's parents to convince them to let their kid try his luck in Kamloops. "I said, 'He's got the athletic ability, and if he works hard, he is going to make it.' Connor had some troubles along the way, but he found his way. He's sort of the classic example of a kid that comes from small-town Saskatchewan. He played all sports."

If Colby Armstrong was all skin and bones at fourteen or fifteen, Ingram, who played AA hockey when he turned sixteen in the winter of 2013, was a little bit more. "He was one of those guys who was probably fifty pounds overweight when he was fourteen or fifteen years old, instead of a string bean. He just kept getting better and better. He was a really good ball player. He was a really good hockey player. He could play any sport, and he kind of started getting himself in shape. He lost some weight. He became an elite goaltender."

Connor Ingram became an NHL goaltender. He went from AA hockey to the best league in the world.

"I always had a bit of a knack for goalies. For me, I always looked at athletic ability. I find it very important. Even if they catch the puck the right way. It's like catching a ball or anything. You can just tell that they are good athletes. To me, I find that's very important with a goaltender," Fox says.

"I did quite a bit of digging when it came to Connor. I said, 'We got to list this kid. He's going to be a goalie.' And it worked out. Lots of times, it doesn't. Sometimes you just got to put yourself on the line and say, 'I'm going to take this guy.' The team trusted what I said, and it went from there. It takes time to establish that trust with a team. It's like working any job. It takes time. You get along with some GMs better than others. You just do. Some guys, whether it's the coach or the GM, you didn't get along. But then the next guy, you hit it off and the trust is there right away. It's been quite a journey."

A journey that started by answering a classified ad.

When Fox was at that game in Phoenix when Ingram played against the Penguins, Sidney Crosby came barrelling down all alone on a breakaway against the one-time AA goalie. Ingram made the save. Fox may be retired, but his mark on the game remains.

"Connor stops him! I mean, that doesn't happen very often, but you kind of stick your chest out a little bit and you're pretty proud. Not that you were a big part of it, but you like to think that maybe you were a bit of it. I've got no regrets. I had lots of fun, and I met lots of good people."

CHAPTER 5

The Long Scouting Road

Grant Sonier

Grant Sonier enjoying his day with the Stanley Cup at his Prince Edward Island home with his wife, Emily, daughter, Ellie, and Ollie the dog. COURTESY GRANT SONIER

Imagine Alexander Ovechkin scoring goal after goal, living life to its fullest on the ice and on the beach—as a Florida Panther. Instead of scoring goal after goal in DC, picture the goals piling up in Miami. It almost happened—kind of. If Florida owner Alan Cohen had had his way, Ovechkin would not have gone number one overall in the 2004 draft. Instead, he would have gone in the ninth round in 2003.

"I'm walking up to make our selection at the draft and [NHL deputy commissioner] Bill Daly sees me coming," says Grant Sonier, who was the Florida Panthers' assistant general manager at the time of the 2003 draft. "He's just shaking his head like 'No way, uh-uh.'"

Cohen had instructed Sonier to go against the ruling of the NHL and pick Ovechkin, who at the time of the 2003 draft was too young to be selected. Ovechkin was born on September 17, 1985. To be eligible for the draft that year, players had to have been born on September 15, 1985, or earlier. The plan, or at least desire, of the Panthers owner had been stoked just a few weeks earlier, after the Panthers' season came to an end.

Cohen had done what he always did. He took the Panthers scouts out for a day on his yacht in South Florida.

"The yacht is like something you see on *Miami Vice*," Sonier begins. "Helipads, hot tubs, Jet Skis. We go out and we have an unbelievable day. But before we went out, our general manager, Rick Dudley, said to me, 'Make sure you talk to the boys and make sure they are really careful about what they say around Alan.'"

Translation: Make sure the boys don't say too much around the boss. Alan was the boss. And as Sonier says, "In the eyes of the hockey world, he wasn't involved, but Alan was involved in the team, as all owners are. It's their money; they should be, I guess."

The "boys" had a great time out on the high seas. There was lots of food and more than enough to drink. After a long season of going from cold rink to cold rink all around the world, what hockey scout wouldn't enjoy a day on the seas of South Florida? As the boat was pulling into the docks, a scout within earshot of Cohen simply mentioned, "Too bad Ovechkin wasn't two days older."

It was an innocent enough comment. If you're wondering why a hockey scout would be talking about hockey on a boat in paradise, well, you don't know too many hockey scouts. They will think and talk about hockey almost anywhere and at any time.

When Sonier heard that innocent comment, he knew he was in for an adventure. "Okay, here we fucking go!" Shortly after that cruise, Cohen hired a lawyer and basically tried to contest the rule about draft eligibility in the NHL's collective bargaining agreement. If you factor in the extra days taken up by leap years, they argued, Ovechkin was eligible for the draft. They were denied. "I don't know how much money Alan spent on this, but he spent a lot of money. He became infatuated with this."

Like most of the civilized world, the NHL recognized the calendar for what it was, and leap years for what they were. No matter how unique Cohen's argument was, or how much he wanted Ovechkin to be eligible for the draft, the answer was no. Alexander Ovechkin could not be taken in the 2003 draft. When draft day rolled around in Nashville on June 21, it went off without a hitch. Marc-André Fleury went first overall to Pittsburgh. Eric Staal went second to Carolina. And when it was time for the Panthers to make the third selection of the day, they followed the rules and picked Nathan Horton. It was all systems go, at least until the time neared for the Panthers to pick in the ninth round.

The Panthers' and Buffalo Sabres' tables were in close proximity. As the eighth round came to a close, Florida GM Rick Dudley and Buffalo GM Darcy Regier were gabbing away, discussing a possible swap of picks. And that's when Dudley's phone rang. It was the owner, Alan Cohen.

"He wants us to pick Ovechkin," Sonier says in amazement.

Now, Rick Dudley, even though this was twenty years after he had last played professional hockey, was still one of the fittest men at the 2003 draft. The man is a workout freak. "I keep telling him he has to slow down in the gym," Sonier says. "He's always got a sore neck. When you get under 255 pounds of weight for a warmup and you start throwing bench presses around at his age, no wonder he's got a sore neck."

And at the 2003 draft, Dudley was a much younger man. He did not like the directive he was getting from his owner to pick Ovechkin, whom the NHL had declared loud and clear was not eligible.

"Duds starts grumbling," Sonier continues, "and the foam starts coming out of his mouth. He slams the phone down. He grabs the table, and he lifts it and he bangs it. Everybody's computer jumped a foot in the air. He pushes his chair back. He leans over to me and says, 'You run the rest of the draft. I'm fucking getting out of here.'"

Dudley got up and left, and Grant Sonier was now in charge of the draft for the Florida Panthers. No one wanted the uber-jacked Rick Dudley on their bad side. "Darcy comes over to me and says, 'Is Duds mad at me?'"

Sonier assured Regier that all was well between him and Dudley, and that for now there would be no deal between the Panthers and Sabres. Next up for Sonier was to take care of the owner—make that owners. The phone rang again, and this time Cohen was on the line along with a couple of the Panthers' minority owners. They wanted the Panthers to select Ovechkin. If Dudley was in a tizzy, too bad. "What do you want me to do?" Sonier said to his owner. "Do you want me to stand up on the table and yell his name out? The mic won't be turned on. We're not taking Ovechkin. Seriously, Alan."

But orders were orders, and the buzz had begun. Sonier says Cohen always had the ear of one of the Panthers' beat writers, and he was floating the Ovechkin story. The media was calling Sonier, too, but he didn't have much time. The Panthers needed to make a selection. When Sonier looked at the back of the draft floor, the assembled media were watching. "There is a buzz going. People know what is going on."

Sonier had to think fast. As teams selected players, they filled out a form, listing details like the name, position and date of birth. The paper would be brought to the front of the draft floor and submitted to league officials. "If the player was eligible to be selected, the league would stamp it and approve it, or [else] they would stamp and reject it," Sonier says.

Sonier filled out a form with Ovechkin's name on it and started his walk to the front of the arena. That's where he ran into a less-than-impressed Daly, with NHL senior vice-president Colin Campbell by his side. Sonier had written Ovechkin's name on the paper, but had no intention of selecting him for the Panthers. He did his best to calm Daly and Campbell down, and then laid out his plan. "I said, 'Guys, I just want you to stamp this rejected so I can take this back to my fucking crazy owner and say I did everything I could.' You know what I mean? I'm trying to cover my ass. I think I'm getting fired."

Boom. The paper was stamped as rejected. Sonier made the not-quite walk of shame back to the Panthers' table and got back to the real work. "We had back-to-back picks, number 264 and number 265. We took Tanner Glass at 265, and the owner wanted us to take Ovechkin."

Tanner Glass was an incredible pick at number 265 overall. Sure, he was no Ovechkin, but he was eligible to be selected, kind of a big deal, and he did play 527 games in the NHL. Not that it mattered to the Panthers' owner at the time. "Cohen tried to fire me. Duds obviously stood up for me."

Sonier survived, and he added a lot of pizzazz to what is usually a pretty dull round of the draft. "I left the draft and I thought I just won an Olympic gold medal. Honest to God, there was more media around me."

They all wanted to know one thing: Did the Panthers really try to draft the Russian teenage phenom? "What's going on?" Sonier remembers the hordes of media asking. "We heard you were taking Ovechkin!"

His answer then was a lot shorter than it is now—it makes for an amazing story today. At the time, though, all Sonier said was "No comment."

That 2003 draft was a long way from where Grant Sonier's hockey career began. He took the long road, the really long road, to the NHL, starting in his native Prince Edward Island. Sonier played junior hockey in Summerside, coached in the Island Junior Hockey League, and then in the Maritime Junior Hockey League when the Summerside Western Capitals joined the mainland loop. Sonier ended up as both coach and GM of the team. After the 1991–92 season, Sonier got his walking papers from the Caps. That's when he got a call from an old pal, Prince Edward Island hockey legend Doug MacLean. MacLean, then an assistant coach with the Detroit Red Wings, was calling about a job opening in Detroit. It wasn't with the Red Wings, though; it was a few rungs down the ladder. Actually, it was as about as far down the ladder as you could get in pro hockey. The Detroit Falcons of the Colonial Hockey League were looking for an assistant coach. Doug gave Grant the name of the head coach, Terry Christensen. Grant called him, and Terry hired Grant over the phone. It was so long PEI and hello Motown—or, more accurately, hello Fraser, Michigan, where the Falcons played, in the Falcon Dome.

"It was the furthest thing from a dome," Sonier says.

The Colonial League had teams in places like Thunder Bay and Brantford, Ontario, and Flint and Muskegon in Michigan. It was not the NHL, not the American League, not the International League, but it was pro hockey. The Falcons were owned by Dr. Khaled M. Shukairy, who owned at least one other team in the league. "I don't know the story of where he came from, but he somehow escaped the country he came from, and I think he escaped with a lot of money."

The league might not have had a lot of different owners, but, like most low minor leagues at the time, it had a lot of different tough guys. One of the Falcons' main pugilists was a guy named Jacques Mailhot. The man they call "The Mailman" had fought his way from the senior ranks in western Quebec and northern New Brunswick all the way to a five-game stint with the Quebec Nordiques in 1988–89. In those five games, he managed to fight Lyndon Byers, Cam Neely and Tim Hunter and collect thirty-three penalty minutes. By 1992–93, when Sonier was his assistant coach, Mailhot was on his way to a team-leading 273 PIMs with the Falcons. The big man had pretty decent hands, too, scoring fourteen goals that year. But most of the time, his hands were used to hurt opponents in a fight.

"I asked Jacques one time in practice, 'What are you doing with your hands?'"

Most tough guys will grab onto an opponent's sweater at the collar or shoulder and twist, but not the six-foot-three, 220-pound Mailhot. "His hands were so big. He used to grab the guys right in the centre of their chest on their jersey and he used to twist. It would pull the guy's arms in and it would restrict them, and he would tee off on them. That's how he won his fights."

If there was blood during a fight, though, that was not a good thing for Mailhot. If the sight of blood fuelled some tough guys, it literally stopped the Falcons' big man. "I don't know if people know this, but he doesn't like the sight of blood. He knocked a guy out one time and he was going back to the penalty box. Jacques looked down and he pulled the guy's tooth out of his hand, and the blood started gushing and Jacques passed out."

The fights and games would take Sonier to all kinds of exotic places on the Colonial League map, like Thunder Bay.

"We used to go up to Thunder Bay and play Friday, Saturday, Sunday. Friday was a brawl, for sure. Saturday, we played hockey, and then Sunday was just an all-out war and the boys would be drinking together at the Golden Nugget. I remember Terry saying, 'We should go check on the guys.' I said, 'I'll go check on them.' They were all at the Golden Nugget with the other team. They had just beat the piss out of one another, and then they're drinking at the Golden Nugget."

A twelve-and-a-half-hour bus ride from Fraser to Thunder Bay could make any pro hockey player or assistant coach ask himself what the hell he is doing with his hockey life. The Detroit Falcons, though, did present Sonier with a hell of a gift. Thunder Bay was 775 miles away, but Joe Louis Arena—home of the Red Wings—was only about half an hour from Fraser. The Falcons were affiliated with the Wings. That was the gift the Falcons gave to Sonier—that, and former Red Wings coach and general manager Bryan Murray. "I was so green back then. Bryan Murray was unbelievable to me. Doug's relationship with him helped. Bryan Murray always invited me down. I was always going to Red Wing games and their practices. When I had time, I was always around the Red Wings. It was awesome."

Grant Sonier was getting his education in hockey. He would spend as much time as he could in the shadows of the Detroit Red Wings coaching staff, listening and learning. "I'm just trying to stay in my lane and not wanting to interfere. Bryan used to invite me into the meetings. I learned so much in that year—just about the operational side of things. As fans, we think we know, but we really don't know what's going on. I was very fortunate."

Sonier got to see up close just what made the great ones so great. "The reason the players are great is because they practise so freaking hard. Steve Yzerman and these guys, they're the best practice players, too. I got my master's degree in hockey hanging out there."

Sonier got to see everything—games, practice habits, even trade demands and how to handle them. "Yves Racine was a defenceman with Detroit. He came in the coach's room—he had half his gear off—and he said, 'Bryan, I need to talk to you. I want a trade.'"

The Wings had just picked up Paul Coffey in a deal. Sonier thought this instant trade request might be too much of a private matter for him to be privy to, so he got up to leave. Murray told Sonier to stay where he was. "Bryan says, 'Don't you fucking ever walk in my office and demand a trade! Don't worry, you'll be fucking gone. Get the fuck out of my office.' And I'm just sitting there. And lo and behold, they traded Racine to Philadelphia two days later."

After his time in Detroit came to an end, Sonier's career took him to Newmarket of the OHL as an assistant coach, to Anaheim in Roller Hockey International, Huntington of the East Coast League and Fort Wayne of the IHL. In the spring of 1999, the NHL finally came calling—or rather, knocking. "I'm coaching in the East Coast League, we are in Toledo one night, and there is a knock at the door.

Toledo was like Johnstown [Pennsylvania]. It was an old-school, old-school arena. I'm in a little closet—that is the coach's office—and there's a knock at the door."

Sonier's team, the Huntington Blizzard, had just finished up a game. And Sonier, the team's head coach, had just spent the night trying to survive. That's what all visiting coaches did in Toledo. "To give you an idea of how crazy that arena is, they had a police officer on our bench next to me. I'm the head coach, and the police officer is facing the fans. There would be beer cans being thrown at us during the games.

"So, I get a knock on my office door after the game," Sonier continued. "The security guard says, 'There is a gentleman by the name of Rick Dudley who would like to talk to you.' I know who Duds is, but I don't know how he knows who I am. So, he puts his big paw out and he shakes my hand. And he says, 'I just want to tell you I've watched a lot of hockey. I love the way your team plays, and if you ever want to talk hockey, let me know.' He gave me his card. He was the GM of the Detroit Vipers."

At the time the Vipers, playing in the IHL, were the top affiliate of the Tampa Bay Lightning. Sonier was flattered, but he did not immediately call Dudley back. As soon as Huntington's playoffs ended, though, Dudley called Sonier.

"We lose in a playoff round, and I get a call the next day from Rick Dudley and he says, 'What's going on?' I said, 'Oh geez, I feel bad. I've been meaning to call you. I've been busy.' He said, 'Don't worry about it.' He said, 'What are you doing?' I told him that we lost last night. He said, 'I know. That's why I'm calling. When you're done doing what you have to do, why don't you come up to Detroit and hang out?' So, I finished my exit meetings and drove up to Detroit. Dudley put me up in a hotel and we literally sat around all day long.

While his team was playing in the playoffs, we travelled together. I flew with the team. We just became friends instantly. He liked the way I coached. He wanted to pick my brain, and subsequently, that's all I did was pick his brain."

The match was made. In early August of 1999, Grant Sonier, just thirty-four, was named the general manager of the Detroit Vipers. His job came with another role as well, as a scout for the Lightning. Grant Sonier was finally in the NHL. From the Island Junior Hockey League to the big time. He made stops in leagues that no longer exist to make it to the best league in the world.

"I remember seeing my first cheque and thinking, *Wow, this is pretty cool.* And Tampa wasn't what they are now. There was a lot of looseness with Tampa. So, what happens is I pay my dues, sure, but I never ever looked at it as paying my dues. I just love the game. I never felt—and even to this day, I never felt I really had to work. You pay the price—you're married, I've got a young daughter. It means you're not home a lot when you're on the scouting side, but that's the price you pay. But I never really felt like I was at work because I love the game."

Sonier stayed in the Lightning organization for a couple of years. He left the Vipers and Bolts when he and Dudley were let go, on the same day. "We were in the car together when we got fired. We were travelling. Jay Feaster called Rick and fired him. My phone rang shortly after, and I was ready for it. I said, 'Just buy me the fuck out. I don't want to wait. You clearly want to get rid of me. Please just give me my money up front so I can go somewhere and continue to work.' And they did!"

Grant wasn't out of work for long. His old buddies and mentors from PEI, Doug MacLean and Jimmy Clark, hired him to scout for Columbus. Rick Dudley was hired to scout for Atlanta. Soon enough, though, Dudley was hired as the new general manager of the Florida Panthers. He didn't take long to hire Sonier, who joined the Panthers staff as assistant general manager just before the 2002 draft. That year, Florida held the first pick, followed by Atlanta, then Columbus and Tampa at four. Dudley and Sonier had just been fired from Tampa Bay. Dudley had briefly scouted for Atlanta. Sonier had briefly scouted for Columbus. Dudley and Sonier were now in charge of the draft for Florida. "We basically know all four team's lists," says Sonier. "I remember Jimmy and Doug [in Columbus] going, 'You better not be divulging!' Now, they could've said, 'No, you can't go until after the draft,' just like Donnie [Waddell in Atlanta] could've said that to Duds, but neither team held us up."

Now in charge of the Panthers' future and armed with the knowledge of how the other teams picking in the top four viewed the prospects for the draft, Sonier and Dudley were in the driver's seat, but how would they go about their business? "Wednesday the week of the draft, we were sitting in Duds's suite. We ordered some pizza and it just dawned on me because we had been going over lists: Why would we ever take Jay Bouwmeester at [number] one overall?"

Bouwmeester was a smooth-skating defenceman out of Medicine Hat of the Western Hockey League. He was everything the Florida Panthers would want as the 2002 draft approached. Florida wanted Bouwmeester badly, but perhaps even more importantly, they knew Columbus wanted someone else: Rick Nash. Dudley and Sonier also knew that Atlanta, who held the second-overall pick, had their eyes on Finnish goaltender Kari Lehtonen—"The best amateur goaltender I've ever seen," says Sonier. But the Panthers had Roberto Luongo in net, so they had no need for Lehtonen.

With that knowledge in mind, the Panthers made their move, swapping picks with Columbus. In exchange, Florida received the option to swap picks with Columbus again in the 2003 draft. Not a huge move, but one that benefited the Panthers and allowed them to get the player they wanted anyway. "We felt the right to flip picks the following year, if we have a decent year and Columbus is still finding their way, we had a chance for a good pick."

The plan worked. Columbus took Nash at number one. Atlanta drafted Lehtonen at two. Florida selected Bouwmeester third overall, rather than first. "We wanted Bouwmeester. We needed Bouwmeester. We knew he was the player we wanted. It's not fair to Bouwmeester, but that was just the business. We thought we could get something for moving to third and the same player."

After two years in Florida, Sonier was on to his next NHL stop. He became head scout of the Los Angeles Kings, working under general manager Dave Taylor. Sonier was at the table—literally kicking—when the Kings picked a huge Slovenian kid named Anže Kopitar eleventh overall at the 2005 draft in Ottawa. This was the Sidney Crosby draft, the one held at the Westin Hotel. Most teams' staffers, as we heard from Brad Davis, were scattered throughout rooms in the hotel. Sonier was at the Kings table, in the process of stealing a future Hall of Famer with the eleventh pick.

Crosby was the consensus number one pick. He was, and still is, a no-doubter to go first overall. He had skated at a Kings camp before (underage players are no longer allowed to be a part of these skates), and when he showed up at the 2005 draft, the Kings went through the motions of interviewing Crosby even though they knew they had no chance of drafting him. Sonier was somehow front and centre when number 87 showed up.

"Sidney came in for an interview with us. Rob Forbes is Sidney's uncle. Robbie and I were at the University of New Brunswick together. When we were at the hotel and the players came in for the combine and the players walked through the door. And me being the eager beaver—I'm right there at the first table. I didn't know that Sidney Crosby knew who I was. Robbie must've given him a picture of me or something. Sid came over and he said, 'My uncle Rob Forbes wanted me to introduce myself to you.' So, the next day in the newspaper it's Sidney Crosby and I shaking hands because the cameras were going off. It was like the paparazzi. And Dave Taylor goes, 'What are you doing? Why is Sidney shaking your hand?' So he came in for an interview, and we go, 'We're picking eleven. We're pretty sure we're not getting you, but we just wanted to say hi to you.' He had been to that camp with us, so David had met him before. And I think some of the scouts might have wanted to get some autographs."

The Kings knew they were not going to get Crosby, but they wanted Kopitar. If you look at the 2005 draft from today's perspective, you could see Crosby going first, followed by Carey Price or Kopitar. Flip those two either way for the logical second or third picks. On draft day, though, Crosby was followed by Bobby Ryan, Jack Johnson, Benoît Pouliot and then Price.

That was good news for the Kings, who had Kopitar at number two on their list. But why did they have him so high? "Everyone questioned Kopitar's skating a little bit. Not a lot, but a little bit. He was a little bit heavy-footed."

The Kings had watched Kopitar a lot. They figured that Kopitar's skating was being questioned because he was such a busy young player. With Södertälje in Sweden, he was shuttling between the junior and senior teams, often playing on back-to-back nights. He was also flying back to his native Slovenia to play for its national teams.

"This guy was all over the place his draft season, and if you caught him on back-to-back games, his skating might've been slightly a little bit more concerning than it was. But we did our homework. Our European staff identified him. Al Murray, our director of amateur scouting, gets over to see him. Al likes him. I end up seeing him a bunch. We just really liked him. I'd go to Europe to see him, I think, maybe three times in total." Dave Taylor also made the trek to see Kopitar.

The Vancouver Canucks were the final team to select before LA. If they passed on Kopitar, the Kings could get the number two player on their list with the eleventh pick in the draft. And at number ten, the Canucks took Luc Bourdon. (The promising young defenceman played in only thirty-six NHL games. He died in a motorcycle accident when he was twenty-one years old.) Kopitar was still available for the Kings. Sonier's feet began to fly.

"I kicked Al Murray so friggin' hard in the shin underneath the table. You could only do that because there were small tables at that draft. We were blown away that we were going to get Kopitar at eleven. Trust me, I'm not the guy who picked Anže Kopitar. We all picked him. The staff picked him. We saw him a lot. I know Al gives me a lot of credit for it. One of the things in scouting is you always want to measure. You want to measure talent versus talent, skating versus skating, character versus character. At the end of the day, impact in a game is really important, and Kopitar impacted games at every level he played at. It was whether he played with the men, whether he played with the national team for Slovenia and certainly junior. He had an impact in various ways on the games he played in. I just had this sense he was going be a great two-way centre."

Kopitar has won two Stanley Cups with the Kings. The kid who was in net for those Cup winners was also taken by the Kings in the 2005 draft: high school goalie Jonathan Quick, stolen at number seventy-two overall. "Brian Putnam [a Boston-based Kings' scout] would've seen him first. Quick went to Avon Old Farms High School. Then he went to UMass after that."

With a goalie so young, how do you scout him? How do you see potential? "Billy Ranford was our goalie coach. We used to bring Bill in to watch some video of the young goalies. One of the things that Brian Putnam didn't like about Quick was that he was all over the place. He was so determined to stop the puck, he often got out of his crease. I had a long conversation with Billy. I said, 'Billy, I look at this differently. If Jonathan is so competitive that he's going so far out of his net to make saves, how good is this guy going to be if we can just get him to play within the parameters of an NHL goaltender?' Billy said [he agreed] one hundred percent. This guy is so athletic and so quick, pardon the pun, quick, so Brian Putnam deserves a lot of credit. We felt very lucky."

Quick and Kopitar were two great picks from the 2005 draft, and important parts of the Kings' Cup championships in 2012 and 2014. By that time, Grant Sonier was no longer part of the Kings organization. He was the general manager of the Charlottetown Islanders of the QMJHL, after NHL stops in Boston and Atlanta.

"What goes through my mind? You know what? I'm proud. Proud that we had something to do with [the Cups]. Al Murray had way more to do with the winning than me. Al Murray was there when they drafted Dustin Brown, drafted Brian Boyle and Jeff Tambellini, which turned into this player and that player. Al was there a long time. And when you get fired, it's quick. It's sometimes thirty seconds on the phone, which makes you bitter. Makes you really bitter."

For a long time, Grant wondered if he would ever get his name on Lord Stanley's Cup. Two years after Tampa Bay let him go, they won it. He worked for the Bruins from 2006 until 2009—then he was let go. They won the Cup in 2011. "There was a point in time where I would just tell people, 'Listen—hire me then fire me, and you're going to win the Cup,'" Sonier says.

Sonier eventually got his Stanley Cup. He started his second tour of duty with the Tampa Bay Lightning in the 2020–21 season. On July 7, 2021, the Lightning beat the Montreal Canadiens, and Grant Sonier was a Stanley Cup champion. "I was in the building when we beat Montreal, 1–0, in Game Five [of the Stanley Cup Final]. I was just really emotional. It was not as emotional as when I had the Cup here [in PEI]. I was bawling all day long."

Sonier hosted the Stanley Cup in Summerside on August 22, 2021. He took it to his local rink, where he started playing as a kid, to the Summerside Boys and Girls Club, to the Summerside Western Capitals' dressing room, to his house—and yes, being a good PEI boy, he invited the neighbours over. "Then I took the Cup to three people. They all died shortly after. Still to this day, I get choked up thinking about it and when I hear their family members talk about that day. Grant Somers was one of the all-time best athletes from PEI; he died of cancer. His mother-in-law was sick, and she died. And my wife is from Brockville. When she moved here, one of the first people she met was a young lady that's married to a friend of mine, Johnny Turner, and she had brain cancer. So, we went down on the water at their place with the Cup. It was something. She knew she wasn't long for the world; she was the happiest person in the world that day."

Sonier spent the winter of 2023–24 out of the game. For the first time in over thirty years, he wasn't hanging out in rinks. "Once you get into scouting, it becomes a little bit contagious. I'm still itching. I still really want back in."

That master's in hockey he earned hanging out with Bryan Murray and the Red Wings staff over thirty years ago was just the start of an education in the game and in the art of scouting that continues.

"The one thing that I've been able to do is evolve. You have to evolve. There are ebbs and flows, and there are trends in drafts. There really is. When Milan Lucic came along, everybody wanted that big, bruising guy. Well, that's fine, but now the little guys are coming and now nobody wants little defencemen. I think you have to evolve. You can fall in love with the US development program. If you watch the under-18 US development program, they all should play in the NHL based on how much skill they have, but you can't fall in love with the skill. Character is non-negotiable. But how do you measure it? Just because they work hard in their own age group, you don't really know how they will do until they get pushed. It's a boy trying to fight against the man until the boy becomes strong enough and learns."

So, what's changed about scouting during Sonier's time in the game? "I think scouting is the same. I think you can't get caught up in all the white noise. The white noise for scouts is all the lists. There used to be one list . . . then there used to be two lists on prospects besides your own list. There are, like, forty of them now. Everybody has a list. It is white noise for scouts.

"I think the other thing that is really, really important—and I know this because I've been fired so much—scouting really, really boils down to what type of player [a team's] management really wants. A guy like [Tampa Bay general manager] Julien BriseBois—and nothing against Julien—but he doesn't want a small defenceman, no matter what. It's almost to the point of just take him off the list. That's just Julien's belief. He believes in big defencemen—and look at the size of the Tampa defencemen. They're all big.

"The hardest thing in the world to do is project. Because you know the player is going to get bigger. You know they're getting stronger. They're going to get faster. Shame on the organization if they can't do those things for their prospects. I think teams are all really good [at development]. Every team has unbelievable resources in terms of strength and mental coaches and all that. So, if the players are given that and it doesn't work out, they probably didn't have the makeup internally to make it."

A scout is just part of the bigger picture. A scout can only recommend and draft. After that, a player's development is out of their hands. "I think I learned early on, and it's really hard: Once the draft is over, you have to emotionally remove yourself from the draft," said Sonier. "It really becomes the development staff's job and the coaching staff's job after the draft. It wasn't like it was 'This player's got no chance—let's take him.' We saw something in him. And again, there are so many moving parts. It's such a fluid situation. We don't really know what's going on in the kid's head. We don't know what's going on in their lives. I mean, things happen from the draft to the first camp. Lots of kids just lose the love of the game because there is such a drive and a push to become better and better and better—and everybody is not built that way."

With that, Sonier adds one more piece of universal scouting wisdom: "I jokingly say I never drafted any bad players. The coaches screwed them up."

CHAPTER 6

Starting from Zero

Gina Kingsbury

Gina Kingsbury has won just about everything in the hockey world, but one of her biggest challenges was putting together a roster for Toronto's PWHL entry in just a few weeks. COURTESY GINA KINGSBURY

If there is one thing that pretty much anyone on the planet wants, it's a clean slate and more time. Gina Kingsbury went one-for-two in that department when she was hired as the first general manager of Toronto's Professional Women's Hockey League team on Friday, September 1, 2023.

"I think the first word that comes to mind is extremely exciting," said Kingsbury. "I think there's very few opportunities in this world to start something from scratch and something that you're passionate about. My favourite part of my job at Hockey Canada was getting involved with the team and naming a team and building a team. Now I get to do this every day with a permanent team that's all-year-round. To me, it's a dream job. It was just really exciting to do it from scratch," says Kingsbury, a two-time Olympic gold medallist as a player and the general manager of Canada's national women's team that won Olympic gold in 2022.

Exciting, Kingsbury says, but there was a major catch. She and the other GMs in the newly formed women's professional circuit were basically without one thing—time. The GMs had ten days to sign three free agents, and then they had to conduct an expansion draft to build their teams. The expansion draft would take place on September 18, leaving less than three weeks to put a team together. "Oh my god. Okay, that's insane. It was, like, three weeks. It was like, 'All right, here you go. You got it.' Wow. So, it was . . . interesting," says Kingsbury. "It was chaotic." Oh, and she had to hire a head coach, too. She went with the head coach of the national team, Troy Ryan, to fill that gig.

To calm the chaos, Kingsbury did what anyone would do: she went with what she knew. As the GM of Canada's national team, she had inside knowledge of the best players Canada had to offer. The three free agents were more than familiar to her. Kingsbury signed Sarah Nurse, Blayre Turnbull and Renata Fast—three members of that 2022 gold medal–winning team. Then it was time for the expansion draft.

"From the scouting perspective, Troy and I basically did the first year completely on our own. There are conversations that you always have with college coaches and coaches that are in the game and people that have a little bit of their finger on the pulse in different leagues and whatnot. There was a lot of conversations with various people, but it was definitely Troy and I sitting down and going, 'Who do we want to build a team around first and foremost? What type of team would we want to have?' We were leaning on our experience and on our knowledge of some of our Canadian players that we knew really well. We knew what they could bring into the locker room. We knew the character that they brought around our team. We knew you could build a franchise and an organization around them. So, yeah, it was definitely Troy and I that did all the heavy lifting for year one. And in a very short window.

"I was with Troy the whole time," says Kingsbury. "So, I felt like we talked—there are twenty-four hours in a day—it felt like we talked probably twenty-six hours a day about the team and what we would do and what would it look like . . . I feel like we've maximized every minute of every day leading into that draft. We were just making sure that we were on the same page. We were both extremely excited about the opportunity—to build a team from scratch and do this every single day in a season. You know, I'm not used to a season; I'm used to a short-term competition and going to a world championship, getting a team together for twelve days. To do that throughout a whole season was really exciting for me. I think we maximized every single minute of every day."

So, what type of team did Kingsbury want? Every team in the league was an expansion team. Do you build to win now? Do you build to win down the road? Kingsbury knew what she wanted to do. "The way the league is set up, it's not necessarily long term. Without a farm system, without the ability to draft someone young and send them down to develop and kind of grow into whatever player you want them to be in the future . . . well, we don't have that right now. So, it's like a now-or-never-type thing. With your team, you want to win right away."

So, Kingsbury and Toronto were in win-now mode heading into the expansion draft. How do you win now? Ultimately, trust won out for Kingsbury and Toronto. Kingsbury had a vast knowledge of the international game. She obviously knew all the players on Canada's greatest rival, the USA, as well, but she knew and trusted those who had played for her on Team Canada. A number of Team Canada's stars, like Marie-Philip Poulin and Brianne Jenner, had been among the eighteen signed in the free-agent period.

Minnesota went young with the first pick of the draft: twenty-three-year-old Taylor Heise, who had just wrapped up her collegiate career at the University of Minnesota. With the second pick in the draft, Kingsbury followed a different path, going with who she knew: a reliable veteran defenceman, thirty-five-year-old Jocelyne Larocque.

Larocque had been there and done that. She had two Olympic gold medals, four World Championship gold medals, and a pro career that stretched back to 2011. "I know we got criticized a bit for taking someone like Jocelyne Larocque so early in the draft because of her age," says Kingsbury. "With our three signings at the start, and then Joss as the second pick overall, you know, it's not that they didn't bring talent and they didn't bring what we needed on the ice.

But what was even more important for us is what they brought off the ice. We were building the foundation and the pillars of an organization that hopefully will have success for many years to come. That was really important to us."

Between Nurse, Turnbull, Fast and Larocque, Toronto's PWHL entry already had its core. Turnbull would soon be named the captain of the team. Larocque and Fast, Canada's number one defence pairing internationally, would anchor the blue line. And Nurse, the leading scorer at the 2022 Olympics, brought plenty of offence up front.

With the fourteenth pick, Kingsbury decided to go with a goalie, Kristen Campbell, who might have been familiar to Kingsbury and women's hockey insiders, but to the casual or even somewhat diehard follower, she was a bit off the board. The former NCAA champion with the Wisconsin Badgers had played a ton in college. In her final season with Wisconsin, 2019–20, she went 24–4–3. The only problem Campbell had was that, since that time, she had hardly played at all. COVID wiped out a ton of hockey. By the time the PWHL expansion draft rolled around, Campbell had played in thirteen games in the PWHPA (Professional Women's Hockey Players Association) and one international game for Team Canada. That's fourteen games in three seasons.

If many hockey onlookers hadn't seen a lot of her, Gina Kingbury had. Campbell was the third-string goalie for Team Canada for three seasons. Ryan and Kingbury saw her on the ice constantly. However, it was only in practice. This is where scouting comes in. What made Kingsbury believe that Kristen Campbell, who played in only fourteen games over three seasons, could bring her practice habits into game action with Toronto?

"You know, she's really technically sound. She's big. She takes up a lot of room. She's extremely dedicated to her craft. Arguably, sometimes too much dedicated to her craft. So, all of those things just indicated to me that she is someone that's going in the right direction," Kingsbury says.

"You see it in practices, you see it in small-space games, that she was, you know, definitely a gamer and with a high, high compete level. All of those things kind of gave you a bit of a gut feeling. It's still a gamble. You never know, right, how players will turn out. But everything indicated that, you know, Kristen would be a really good one to go after. And so we knew that that was the goalie we were kind of targeting. And we also knew she was a bit of a dark horse in the sense where, you know, we could wait a little bit in the draft, and she probably wouldn't be taken. And we would be able to pick her up a little bit later and still get the goalie we wanted."

The pick worked. Campbell led the PWHL with sixteen wins in its first season. She was also tops in shutouts, with three, and second in goals-against average at 1.99. "I think there's a really high ceiling with her, I think she's just scratching the surface right now as we speak. We were just confident that with time, she'd become one of the best goalies in the world," says Kingsbury.

Everyone knew the player Toronto took with the twenty-third pick, Natalie Spooner. Looking back, it is almost shocking that Spooner wasn't selected until the fourth round of the expansion draft. Superstar: check. Sniper: check. Great personality: check. Marketable: check—she had already won Olympic gold and appeared on *The Amazing Race Canada* and *Battle of the Blades*. She was a well-known commodity in the game. Spooner was also a new mom. She gave birth to her son, Rory, nine months before the expansion draft. Toronto got a little help with this one. Spooner had applied to the league for a compassionate circumstances waiver. Spooner wanted to remain close to Toronto, where she and her husband and young son lived. "The draft had a few stipulations around some players, and she was one of them. So, it was a little bit out of our control. And that was kind of where she fell."

Spooner landed perfectly in Toronto's lap. She led the league with twenty goals. "Obviously, she's very offensively driven," said Kingsbury. "She is probably one of the players that is really hungry and enjoys scoring more than anybody else. I think everyone enjoys scoring, but for her, it's like it's a deep-rooted passion. She's obsessed with scoring. Did she exceed my expectations? One hundred percent. I don't think anyone would have predicted the type of year that she had, but we knew we would get offence out of her for sure, and we definitely did. But she definitely had a year that was probably beyond what we would have predicted."

The core of Toronto's team—the three free agents and their first four picks in the expansion draft—was suddenly comprised of reliable, mostly veteran players. The average age of the first seven players on Toronto's roster was almost twenty-nine. "I know we got criticized on some of the picks, maybe our choices in terms of age," Kingsbury says. But she would do it again.

Even though Kingsbury had been on the job for less than three weeks, she had been scouting these players for years.

"Obviously, we picked really familiar people. We got criticized a little bit for that as well. With the timelines that we had, you're going to go with what you know. When I look back at the season, we were pretty on par with what we thought would happen with the players that we picked, in terms of who would have success and who would be carrying the team. Again, the biggest focus for us is that we got a chance of building something from scratch. So, you don't want to have to go back in year two and fix some of the cracks that you've created. The character, the type of people that we brought in, was really, really important to us."

The plan worked—at least for the regular season. After a slow start, with only two wins in their first seven games, Kingsbury's squad caught fire and won eleven games in a row. By the end of the regular season, they were at the top of the PWHL standings with forty-seven points. Everything was going according to plan. They met Minnesota in the first round of the playoffs and won the first two games, but then in Game Three, it all went bad. The league's leading scorer, Natalie Spooner, was cruising along in front of Toronto's bench with her team down 2–0 in the third when she took a hit from Minnesota's Grace Zumwinkle. It was clear right away that Spooner had hurt her knee. She crawled to the open door to Toronto's bench. She was done for the playoffs and her knee needed surgery. Minnesota won Game Three, then took Games Four and Five, too. They came back from a 2–0 series deficit to beat the PWHL's top regular-season team. Kingsbury's first season as GM was over.

"Did we have gaps in our team?" Kingsbury asks herself. "Absolutely. I think everyone had gaps; you had no choice but to have gaps. There are maybe a few decisions that I would have done maybe a little bit differently, or a few different picks. I would have loved to have more time to maybe take a little bit more chances on players that we didn't know as well. I think the last part of our draft was also people we knew, which was good, and we felt comfortable with it. But maybe it would have paid off more to take a little bit more of a chance or gamble on players at that stage. I think more research and . . . a little bit more diving into each player [would have helped]. But looking at our season, I'm really happy with what we had and what we were able to accomplish."

Kingsbury continued, "You know, us falling short, I don't think was necessarily roster-driven. Would we have liked to have more offence? I think the big question when Natalie went down was: Will the offence come? I don't think that was necessarily the case. I think we had a bad game—a really shitty game [in Game Five], to be quite honest with you. You lose someone like Spooner, it's not just losing the player or what she does or brings on the ice. It also rattles the team in some ways."

But with the season over, that just means a GM had to get working on the next one. As Kingsbury mentioned, she and Troy Ryan had handled most of the scouting during Toronto's first season. And that included scouting for the PWHL's first entry draft, which took place on June 10, 2024. That work had begun almost as soon as the expansion draft, nine months earlier, had ended, and Kingsbury was the head bird dog at this draft, too.

"Troy can run our entire organization easily if I'm not around. I did miss games to catch NCAA games. I did travel quite a bit to see players and even to be seen. There's an important aspect to that as well. You can get video clips of every game, you can get stats on people, you can do a lot of scouting online, but there's something to be said when an athlete looks up in the stands and goes, 'Toronto's here,'" said Kingsbury. "I think that is really impactful. Any impressions you have on these athletes go a long way. And women's hockey is such a small, quaint, very small group of people. So, impressions are really important. Because that athlete that you may not pick up and draft this time around, but has seen you in rinks and has a lot of respect for you and all of that, may come back as a free agent and may want to play in Toronto someday. So, I think that's really important," says Kingsbury.

That first year on the road was also a chance for Kingsbury, a product of St. Lawrence University, to establish relationships with NCAA coaches and set up a pipeline to Toronto. "It's also important to build relationships with the coaches in the NCAA. It's one thing to call them and ask for favours—'Hey, what do you think about this player, can you tell me about these players, or can I steal an hour of your time to chat?' They're more likely to do that if they see that you're putting the effort in to come and watch their teams, and to show up at their practices. I think that's really important. So, I did that quite a bit this year."

Along with scouting college games, Kingsbury kept an eye on international play. When all her scouting work was in the books, Kingsbury and Toronto made a list of the top sixty prospects for the entry draft. And then Kingsbury started making virtual calls—sixty of them. "I thought, hey, maybe it'll be a half an hour conversation with each player. I'll get to know them a little bit better. I'll get to introduce Toronto to them. I'll get them comfortable. This is new for them as well. They're all curious on what this league is all about and what the expectations are for them. I was surprised. I don't think there was a call that was under an hour. So that ended up being quite the task—sixty ninety-minute conversations with up-and-coming athletes. I just thought it was really, really valuable to get to know them a little bit, but also even just sharing what our culture is and what to expect if they did come to Toronto. I knew that we would only get seven out of those sixty players, but you were leaving an impression on them. There are fifty-three players that you don't get to draft but hopefully you can leave a good enough impression so if they are ever free agents, they'll be curious about wanting to be in Toronto. Again, that's your only opportunity to leave an imprint, to get a conversation going with these athletes, until they're free agents."

Unlike in the past in the NHL where it could be a prospect in front of up to a dozen or so scouts, Kingsbury did things one on one. Think of an NHL prospect, interviewed by a legendary GM, many of whom are Hall of Famers. That could be intimidating. Well, these young players were also being interviewed by a legend in Kingsbury, a two-time Olympic gold medallist. Chances are most of these prospects grew up watching Kingsbury play. Kingsbury in no way wanted the prospects to be intimidated by her.

"In today's game and with today's athletes, there's definitely not as much of a hierarchy as maybe there used to be like. You know, I'm still scared shitless of Mel Davidson [her former coach on the national team]," she laughs. "Nowadays, there's no advantage to have a little bit of that kind of fear. Intimidation, it's definitely not my personality. To me, the interviews were fifty-fifty. And I said that right off the bat. That was kind of my opening line, that it's important to us to bring the right people into our organization, so I want to get to know them as well as I possibly can."

"Don't kid yourself," she told the players. "You should be asking me questions and getting to know what we have to offer and what we don't have to offer, so that you've got a good landscape of what each market looks like. Because one day you'll be in the driver's seat, and you'll be able to tell your agent, 'Hey, call Gina. I would like to see if Toronto has an opportunity for me.'"

Kingsbury felt that it was key to share what Toronto's personality was like, what the culture looked and felt like. She "even put in some expectations. One of the questions I asked was, 'What do you expect from us?' I want to be able to meet your expectations as an athlete. I want to make sure that we have the right pieces to make sure that you're happy and content with what you're receiving back from us. It's not just a paycheque. Do you want to grow? Do you want to learn more? What are the things that you want from us? At the same time, here's our expectations as well when you come to Toronto."

And Kingsbury took in more than just what the prospects said to her. She watched their body language as well. "You get to see if they lean in. I think I mentioned that in one of my interviews after the draft. You could tell the athletes that leaned in. You could see if athletes did or didn't really connect with what you were saying. You kind of knew if they were excited or not, or if they would be the right fit. I like that."

There was also an elephant in the room for Gina Kingsbury to address. She wanted to let American players know that if they came to Toronto, they were playing for Gina Kingsbury in Toronto, that she wore the Toronto hat in Toronto, not the Canadian national team hat. Yes, she was still the GM of Canada's national team, but if you played in Toronto, she'd have your back. She wanted to make clear that her Team Canada role would have no impact on how she would treat any non-Canadian players when they came to play for her club team in the PWHL.

"It was important for me to establish with American players that we want them to be successful. And that we're the type of people that separate [Toronto and Team Canada] very well. Troy will work really hard at getting you to be the very best you can be, not only for Toronto, but if your aspirations are of winning a gold medal at the Olympics, then we will help you be as good as you can be. That is our job—to make you as good as you can be. We take pride in that. There's no favouritism. There's no 'Okay, we'll work with our Canadian players.' If you come to Toronto, we're all in and we want to make sure that you're supported and get what you want out of your career, not just with Toronto, but with your national team, even though you're going to go against us at Worlds. We'll change your hat at Worlds, and best of luck and off you go. That was really important, and you need to have those conversations."

With their first pick in the entry draft, sixth overall, Kingsbury looked to her alma mater, selecting Julia Gosling from St. Lawrence

University. Kingsbury says the university connection had nothing to do with the pick. Once again, she knew the player well through Hockey Canada. Gosling first represented Canada at the Under-18 Worlds in 2018 and ultimately worked her way up to the senior national team at the 2024 World Championships. She led St. Lawrence in scoring in her senior year, with fifty-one points in thirty-seven games in 2023–24. She and the other six Toronto draft picks (two Canadians, three Americans and one Czech) will help add to the core already established by Kingsbury in a wild first year for Toronto's PWHL entry.

"Yeah, I think the sky's the limit. That's the fun part. Where do we take this next, and what's the next step? I think that is exactly why it's so exciting to start a league from scratch, a team from scratch. As much as I'm sure everyone knows that there's been some challenges, it's never perfect. But where you can take it and how you can build onto it. That is really, really exciting.

"Of course, I think, *Hey, wouldn't it be great to have a farm system?*" Kingsbury continues. "And now, to be able to draft players and strategically think that they'll be ready in five years' time. We'll put them in the right system, and we'll do the right things for their development." Kingsbury is a roll. You can feel her passion as she dreams aloud of what her team and this league could be.

"And hiring someone to manage all that—a director of player development—and putting all the pieces together, it's exciting to see it grow. Even in year two, we are expanding a little. We've got more staff coming in. We're already building a little bit more than we did in the first year. To be a part of building it all and the vision of what it could look like is pretty exciting. Seeing other established sports and what they do, but tweaking it to fit into what and who we are in Toronto and what our needs are and what it looks like. That is very cool. So, I don't take it for granted. I'm pretty appreciative of the opportunity."

Kingsbury is also not taking for granted that, even though she does not have enough time, she at least has more than three weeks to plan for the upcoming season and seasons ahead. Now, she's looking way on down the road.

"I spent a good chunk of the summer after the first year thinking of all the different ways our organization can get better and where we're heading and what it looks like. What it will look like in 2026. Who's coming out of college in 2027? Who's replacing Renata Fast when she'll be done and retiring? Who's replacing Spooner when she'll be done? I'm just looking further ahead in the future—who's coming up and how can we make sure that we sustain our success for many years to come?"

The work, for Kingsbury, will continue. Unlike in year one, she won't be getting a fresh start, but she will be working with a little more time.

CHAPTER 7

Trading in the Stripes

Wayne Mundey

Wayne Mundey with the Stanley Cup.

"He was two feet away and he was staring right at me," remembers former St. Louis Blues scout Wayne Mundey.

One of Wayne's favourite expressions is "You don't find hockey. Hockey finds you." Long before Wayne Mundey became an NHL scout, on that October night in 1973 in Edmonton, Mr. Hockey found him.

It all started when an Edmonton Oilers player, Jim Harrison, who would go on to WHA fame by scoring ten points in a single game, took a run at Mark Howe. Mark was one of three Howes on the Houston Aeros, along with his brother Marty and his dad, Gordie—aka Mr. Hockey, who had come out of retirement to play with his sons. Mundey, just twenty-four years old back in 1973 and refereeing his first WHA game, put his arm in the air when he saw Harrison deliver an elbow to the back of Mark Howe's head. This meant the Aeros were going on the power play. When the Oilers touched the puck, Mundey blew his whistle. Harrison was getting two minutes for elbowing. Mundey did his thing.

"You never turn your back to the play as an official," says the more than likeable Montrealer. "You always make sure that you skate backwards towards the penalty box. So, I'm skating backwards towards the penalty box, and I look, and of course the old man—he hits Harrison."

You can probably guess who "the old man" was. Mundey didn't hesitate. Like just about everyone on the ice that night, he'd grown up watching Gordie Howe during his days with the Detroit Red Wings. But in that split second, he wasn't watching the great Gordie Howe. He was simply doing his job as an official, trying to keep law and order between the Aeros and Oilers. Mundey took one look at

Howe and shouted, "And you!" Mundey was sending Gordie Howe to the penalty box.

"Gordie turns and he comes right at me. Eyes staring at me, he looks right at me, and he said, 'Mundey, guys like you will kill this league!' I went back to my faceoff, put my hands down on my knees . . . and I thought, *Oh my God, I'm done.* 'Mundey, guys like you will kill this league.' I will never forget it."

Wayne Mundey did not, in fact, kill the WHA; a lot of other factors did. Mundey stayed with the rebel league right up until the end, when it merged with the National Hockey League in 1979. Years before, Mundey had been like a lot of players in the hockey world: under contract to the NHL, but as an official. When the WHA came around, the league didn't just comb the NHL and AHL for players—it wanted officials, too.

"I always wanted to be an official. I remember going to a junior game in Montreal with my dad. I must've been sixteen or seventeen. There were eighteen thousand people in the old Forum. I was looking, and I saw these three guys come out on the ice. It was the officials in the warmup. I had played a little bit, like everybody did, and I looked down to the ice and I thought, *That is what I want to do.* It was almost like if you want to be a policeman or sports announcer, you have this focus and you just kind of stay with it. I ended up going to referee schools in Haliburton, Ontario. Bruce Hood [a long-time NHL ref] had a school up there. Vern Buffey [also an NHL ref] had a school up there. I went two summers in a row. Scotty Morrison [then the NHL's referee-in-chief] was there. They were looking for officials, and I was fortunate. One of the things I could do was skate. It's a prerequisite, obviously, so I wasn't a bad skater. We had relay races; I'd end up second or third and that would kind of give me a leg up."

Mundey eventually signed on with the NHL, but he worked primarily in the AHL. That all changed when he took that WHA deal. He was part of a hockey adventure, a hockey odyssey, for the rest of the 1970s. "I really enjoyed the WHA. I was on the ice with Bobby Hull and Gordie Howe. It was just amazing to be on the ice with those guys."

Mundey also shared the ice with some of hockey's most notorious men while he tried to call the rule book in hockey's newest major league. For every Howe or Hull, there was a Steve Durbano or Gord Gallant. The WHA produced some beautiful hockey—the high-flying Winnipeg Jets trio of Bobby Hull, Anders Hedberg and Ulf Nilsson, known as the Hot Line, set the stage for the high-flying Edmonton Oilers of the 1980s. But the WHA could also be violent. Very violent. It was up to Mundey and his officiating partners to manage a game, to keep each night under control, as best as they could. "If I was reffing a game and I had a guy like Gordie Gallant playing, guys that were completely off the wall, I would try and get them early. I'd give them a shitty penalty just to settle them down. And a guy like Gallant, he knew he was in that league just to do that."

One night, Gordie took a run at Gordie. As in Gallant, who finished third all-time in WHA career penalty minutes, took a run at Gordie Howe. "Gallant left his skates and everything like that. I called the penalty."

Howe didn't retaliate; he just let it slide. Howe was much bigger than Gallant, but revenge was not on his mind. Mundey wondered why. On the way out of town after the game, Mundey ran into Howe at the airport. "I said, 'Gordie, I'm wondering why didn't you do something to that guy.'"

Howe looked at Mundey and told him something that stuck with him for all these years: "'I won't do it because all he needs to do is get one lucky punch in on me and I go down and he's a hero.' That was pretty sharp of the old man. I mean . . . he'd clean Gallant. But he said if Gallant got a lucky punch in, the headline would be GORDIE GALLANT KNOCKS OUT GORDIE HOWE! I thought that was quite observant of Howe."

Mundey earned a lifetime of lessons as a WHA official. He didn't know it then, but those lessons would set him up for life about twenty years after the merger. When the NHL and WHA merged in June 1979, dozens of players entered or re-entered the NHL. However, only four referees made the jump. Mundey was not one of them. His officiating career was over, in an instant.

"I got a call from my boss. He said, 'Wayne, I don't know what to tell you.'"

Mundey started a career in sales back home in Montreal. That's where he stayed for almost twenty years, until an old friend came calling.

Larry Pleau was a rare breed in the 1960s. He was an American kid playing junior hockey for the Montreal Junior Canadiens. Pleau eventually turned professional and spent some time with the Montreal Canadiens and their farm clubs before doing what Mundey did in 1972—jumping to the World Hockey Association. Just like Mundey, Pleau was in the WHA from its start in the fall of 1972 until its death in June of 1979. And like Mundey, Pleau, who spent his entire WHA career with the New England Whalers, did not continue his playing career in the NHL. When the merger took place, Pleau put his skates away. The key difference between the former player and the former referee is that Pleau did jump to the NHL, as a coach. He went from WHA Whaler forward in 1978–79 to NHL Whaler assistant coach for the 1979–80 season. Pleau served in coaching and front-office roles with the Whalers and New York Rangers for the next twenty or so years, while his old buddy Wayne was back in Montreal.

Towards the end of the 1990s, Larry Pleau became the general manager of the St. Louis Blues. He had a chat with Wayne. Mundey had never played at the pro level, but had shared the ice with the best at the pro level. He knew what it meant. He knew the players. It was in his blood. At one time, Wayne Mundey's dad was even a scout for the Philadelphia Flyers. Now Wayne's friend Larry, whom he had known for thirty years, was offering him a job as a scout for the Blues.

"When Larry hired me, he said, 'Do you want to stay in the business?' I said, 'I'd love to.'"

Mundey started on the amateur side, scouting the Quebec Major Junior League, hoping to find that next great St. Louis Blue. There was a learning curve, but Mundey had seen the game for years, and for a decent amount of that time from a unique perspective, as an official.

"There was a transition. In my opinion, I think if you want to be a scout, I think at some point you had to be on the ice as an official or a player, just to feel the pulse of the game. That's just my opinion. There are guys who are doing great work in the scouting world that have never been on the ice."

Mundey, being a wise old ref, wanted to keep his eyes open. And the wise old ref, new to the scouting world, latched onto a man he and everyone else in the hockey world called Foxy, Bill Dineen. Dineen was a hockey lifer. He played in the NHL in the Original Six era, played for years in the minors, was a head coach in the NHL, WHA and AHL, and by 1998 was a sixty-six-year-old scout with the St. Louis Blues.

"I made sure that I focused on the right people. One guy who really helped me was Bill Dineen. His experience spoke for itself. He had this way of explaining a player. You would sit in a meeting and Bill would explain a player in a minute and a half. And I'd think, *Wow.* After the games, on the bus, I'd sit beside Bill and say, 'Listen, I don't know about this guy. I don't think his skating was as good as you said.' He would say, 'Wayne, there's a difference between speed and pace.' And he told me why it mattered. He would teach me the scouting business. God, I love the man. If I have one person that I would say made me a scout, I would say it was Foxy. He was just fantastic."

Mundey picked up bits of advice early in his scouting career wherever he could. "When I first started to scout, I ran into a scout from Los Angeles. We were sitting in a bar somewhere and I said, 'Yeah, I just started. Can you give me any advice?' And he said, 'Wayne, I'll give you the best advice anybody can give you.' 'What's that?' 'Go to games.' I didn't quite digest it right away. He meant: If you go see a player six times, he is not going to fool you. And it's stuck with me."

It also means, sometimes, having to let go. Put another way, sometimes the first impression is incorrect. If you fall in love with a player the first time you see him, you have to be able to let it go if he didn't give you a reason to keep believing in him. "That's where we get back to seeing a player six times. That's why scouts work so hard. We never stop. We see two hundred–plus games every year. You have to do that."

And once you see a player enough, and you form an opinion on them, stick with what you have seen. Stick to the conclusion you have arrived at. Stick with your convictions. You can't fold under questioning. "You can't do that. That is the biggest no-no for GMs. You have to stay with your convictions."

The Blues usually met three times a year as a staff—once before Christmas, once before the trade deadline and once before the draft. Mundey figures it took him about two seasons before he got his sea legs, before he got that confidence that every scout needs. It took him two years before he could sit in a meeting with other scouts and speak confidently about what he saw in a player. Every profession has its learning curve—be it player, referee or scout.

"David Perron was the one that I really pushed for. I'm not saying I'm the only reason we drafted Perron, but I stuck with him. I really liked what I saw."

Mundey eventually moved to the pro side of the scouting department for the Blues. He was no longer out to discover the next great prospect for St. Louis. He was now looking at players already in the pros. Who would be a good young pro to throw in as part of a trade? Were there any unheralded players out there, someone overlooked, who the Blues may have interest in?

Alexandre Burrows never became a Blue, but Mundey still recalls the first time he saw him skating in the ECHL. "I liked him a lot. I could see the upside, his work ethic. What I look for, and a lot of scouts look for, is heart. That you cannot coach. Players either have it or they don't. I look as heart as a skill. I'm talking first on puck. You don't check with your eyes, as Hitch [long-time coach Ken Hitchcock] said. I love that expression. That's a big thing, and then from there, obviously, there's your skating, your hockey sense. But for me, heart is the first skill I look for."

Another big date on the hockey calendar is the trade deadline. You'll hear about a dozen scouts or more checking out a potential trade target as the deadline nears. In the winter of 2023, dozens of scouts were following the Calgary Flames as the NHL's trade deadline neared. They wanted to get an up-close look at veteran defenceman Chris Tanev, who was a prized piece on the trade market.

"The GMs are the ones making the final decisions. The GM is saying, 'I wonder how he is playing.' You are there to get a very current evaluation on that player. The next morning, you send in your report, and it goes right to the GM."

What goes into his reports? "My reports at trade deadline are about the present, never the past or the future. How is he playing right now? Can he help us win right now?"

And there is a bonus about being at a game with a lot of other pro scouts lurking around the press box and at the pre-game meal. "A lot of times, you can get scoops in the press room. We all eat together. We're all pretty good with each other. Sometimes, I'd sit with a guy, and I'd say, 'Did you see so-and-so the other night?' And he'll say, 'Yeah, I was in Detroit, and I didn't like him, maybe something is wrong with him.' We all travel together after the game. You say, 'Where are you going? Are you going to Toronto? Yes? Let's go.' We're all pretty open . . . but within reason. We wouldn't necessarily say, 'Hey, by the way, we are definitely trading for X on Monday.'"

After a couple of decades with the Blues, Wayne Mundey got to where all hockey people want to get: the Stanley Cup Final. The Blues were led in the spring of 2019 by Jordan Binnington in goal. Binnington had spent half of that season in the AHL. Injuries opened up a spot for him in the lineup and he ran with it. With Mundey and the scouts scattered around the hockey world, Binnington and the Blues found themselves in the second round against the Dallas Stars. The series went the distance. With a nervous Mundey glued to his TV, Game Seven went into double overtime.

There's a moment from that game that still sticks with Mundey. It's the moment that pops into his head when I bring up the Blues' run to their first and only Stanley Cup championship.

"Binnington obviously was amazing. I'm thinking of Game Seven in Dallas, when Jamie Benn came around in OT and tried to sneak it by Binnington on the short side. If he didn't stop that, we would've been out."

Binnington was a call-up who got a chance. He saved the season for the Blues with that quick stop on Benn. A month later, the Blues ended their season with a Stanley Cup. And that's the way Wayne Mundey ended his NHL career. He went out in style. "For the finals, they brought us in, and we travelled with the team. It was amazing."

Mundey was part of the St. Louis Blues scouting staff for twenty-two seasons. He didn't retire from hockey, though. He now serves as senior advisor for the Saint John Sea Dogs of the QMJHL. He won a Memorial Cup with them. He is still in the rinks for the Sea Dogs, and still happy to talk hockey wherever and whenever.

"I was flying down to Florida recently, and there was a team from the East Coast Hockey League in the airport. They were going out to Newfoundland to play the Growlers. You know me, I'm not shy. I said hello."

As the conversation went on, the players learned that they were talking to a Stanley Cup champion. They were talking to a guy who spent over two decades as a scout with the St. Louis Blues. In other words, they were talking to the very type of guy they were hoping to impress. "Within ten minutes, there were about fifteen guys around me. I told them exactly what I just told you. I said, 'Don't give up. One thing that I want to stress to you is heart. Second efforts.' Just make sure if I'm sitting up in the stands, that when I look down, I see something different. Otherwise, you just blend in. I have to look down there and think, 'Look at 17! I'm going to watch him a little more.' I'll stick with him for maybe three or four shifts. But if you're not doing anything, and there's no second effort—or no first effort—or anything like that, and you're not playing hard, you will just blend in. And if you blend in, chances are you won't be in my report."

Mrs. Mundey, who was somewhat patiently waiting for her husband to wrap things up so they could get on with their travels, may not have enjoyed the impromptu airport hockey pep talk, but the players did. Wayne was just being himself. Wayne Mundey wanted to make his mark in the game as an official. He did. But he has lived the last quarter century of his life as a scout. He's the first to admit he got the job because of his good friend Larry. But he didn't hang around for the last twenty-five years because of their friendship.

"When Larry said, 'Do you want to stay in the business?' I said of course I do. He just told me, 'See if you like it. Let's see where it goes.' The more I got into it, I realized how valuable scouting was to the GM. I learned how important scouting is for the draft, to make sure you have a feel for the players, where you ranked them. The more I got into it, I saw the older guys were so efficient at it, and I wanted to get to that point, too. I fell in love with scouting because I saw how valuable it was to your GM."

When Wayne Mundey wanted to be a ref, he put in extra work at referee schools in the summer run by the likes of Bruce Hood. Scotty Morrison eventually found Mundey. A few years after that, the WHA found Mundey. After a twenty-year hiatus, the NHL, via Larry Pleau, found Mundey again. Sure, Pleau wasn't searching for a player; he was searching for a scout. But if you're good enough, be it as a scout or a player, as Mundey learned a long ago, the game will find you.

"You don't find hockey. Hockey finds you. And that is something that a lot of parents should think about. Players don't fall through the cracks anymore. Players are scouted across the world. Believe me, if you can play, you are going to be found."

And if you can scout, hockey will find you, too.

CHAPTER 8

On the Job Training

Jeff Twohey

Jeff Twohey (right) and one of his old players with the Petes, Chris Pronger, sharing a moment with the Cup after Chris won hockey's most storied prize. COURTESY JEFF TWOHEY

Have you ever hitchhiked? Have you ever strolled along the highway, thumb out, hoping, praying, that someone will be kind enough to pick you up and take you on down the road? I have. I was desperate to get home from Wolfville, Nova Scotia, so my dad could truck me off to college the next day. The old man had hitchhiked through Europe and told me if a thumb was good enough for him, then it was good enough for me. The thumb worked. I did safely make it home to Pictou that day.

Maybe you needed to get to school. Maybe you needed to get to a friend's place.

Jeff Twohey needed to get to a hockey game.

Twohey was a student at Laurentian University in 1980. While at school, he had been scouting the Sudbury area for the Junior A Aurora Tigers. Then he put a call in to Dave Dryden, who was head coach of the Peterborough Petes. Twohey figured the OHL franchise might want to have a set of eyeballs in the Sudbury area. Dryden agreed. He brought on Twohey as a part-time scout. And that's how Twohey found himself, thumb up, on the side of the road. He was on a scouting mission for the Peterborough Petes. He was a scout without a car. That didn't matter to the kid at all; he had a game to get to.

"There were times that I'd hitchhike. There were times that I borrowed a car. It was never an issue. Scouting was something I really loved to do. I was just finding a way to do it."

Soon enough, Twohey, who had dreamt of a life as a hockey player until an injury derailed his plans during his OHL draft year, graduated from Laurentian. He was determined to have a life in hockey—but how? Twohey got word that an OHL team was in the market for an assistant GM. He got an interview. It went well. "It sounded like I was getting the job. They called me a couple of days later, and they said they didn't have the budget. They were not going to go with an assistant general manager. It devastated me. I thought, *What am I going to do?* But it was the best thing that ever happened to me."

Why? Because a short time later, Twohey got a call from Dick Todd, who had taken over from Dave Dryden in Peterborough. Todd had an offer for Twohey. Todd, who'd got his break as a trainer behind the Petes bench in the early 1970s, wanted to know if Twohey would like to get his start the same way, and he could scout as well. "Trainer/scout" sounded perfect to Twohey, who, if you're curious, didn't have a second of medical training when he accepted the job. If you were brave enough to hitchhike, you were brave enough to deal with the scars and scrapes of the Ontario Hockey League.

"Back then, you didn't really need to be qualified. I had a friend of mine that was a chiropractor who was really into fitness. He taught me a lot about injuries, just the basics. I kind of taught myself how to tape guys up, whether it was an arm or a wrist. I taught myself how to sharpen skates, how to fix equipment."

In the OHL in the early 1980s, "trainer" also meant you were the equipment manager. So, young Twohey, fresh out of Laurentian, suddenly had a lot on the go—trainer, equipment guru, scout—and he could handle mostly anything that his new job(s) threw at him. But he could not handle one thing: He would not stitch a guy up.

"We had a team doctor. The doctor was an older guy. He was a really good man. He was good to me. It got to the stage where he said, 'Jeff, I'm going to show you how to stitch. You can do it. I don't need to be running down here all the time every time somebody gets cut.'"

The doc may have wanted to cut down on his steps, but Twohey didn't care. Stitches, at least putting them in, were off-limits. "I said, 'Jesus Christ! I really don't want to do that.' I rejected that opportunity. But I was really good at taking [the stitches] out."

Stitches were a big part of the game in the OHL. (They still are.) But they were a really big part of junior hockey in the 1980s. Brawls weren't so much the exception as the rule. Twohey was only a couple of years older than the players he was taking care of, and the ones he was taking shots at on the other team. You know that old footage you see of the trainers being just as big a part of the action as the players? It's true.

One time, the Petes and Oshawa Generals had a bench-clearing brawl. "I was pretty mouthy," remembers Twohey. "I had had a couple warnings from the league about a couple of things that happened, and we were in Oshawa one night and they had said some things about us in the paper. Dick Todd started our five toughest guys. A brawl broke out. Our benches were beside each other, which got me involved. It was my own fault. Just stupidity, really. I got filled in by a couple of players."

Translation? A couple of Generals players had their way with Twohey and put a decent beating on him. Then OHL commissioner David Branch did as well. He suspended Twohey for ten games. "I said to Dave, when he announced his retirement, 'You gave me a record that I don't think could ever be broken. What trainer would ever be suspended for ten games?'"

There were other incidents, too, like the time Twohey wanted a piece of Larry Mavety, the head coach of the Belleville Bulls. Mavety had played pro hockey throughout the 1960s and '70s. The man they called Mav was even an extra in the movie *Slap Shot*. Needless to say, he could handle himself.

On the surface, at least, that was not enough to calm Twohey, who wanted a piece of Mavety one night on the road. At least, it looked like he wanted a piece of him. Mavety had jumped between the benches, trying to get at Twohey. Dick Todd, the head coach of the Petes, grabbed a hold of Twohey to rein him in.

"Todd had a hold of me and he's screaming in my ear, 'What the fuck are you doing?' I told him, 'I don't know. But don't let go!' Mav became a very good friend of mine as time went on. I got to know him. I miss him a lot. He was a really good person. We had a good friendship. Maybe he respected me. It looked like I wasn't backing down, but in fact, I kind of was backing down. I didn't want a part of Mav."

Most nights after a night like this, Twohey would tidy up the Petes room, and if the Petes were off the next day or night, he'd hit the road to go on a scouting trip. He had his own car at this time, so he didn't have to hitchhike anymore.

"It wasn't easy. We'd play on a Thursday night. I'd stay until one or two in the morning and have everything ready for practice the next day. If we weren't playing, then I'd be gone, we'd have an assistant come in and everything was ready for him, and he'd get through practice. It was never a burden. Sometimes I think, *Was I stupid?* But I never complained. I always felt I was very fortunate."

Twohey and Jacques Martin, then an assistant coach with the Petes, would bird-dog from rink to rink. In the mid-1980s, things were different. What a scout was looking for then was far different than what a scout is looking for now. Remember, Twohey saw—and at times felt—the effects of tough-guy '80s hockey up close.

"Back then, in the early eighties, you were looking for size and toughness. It was a priority, maybe overshadowing skill to a certain extent. It was almost an arms race in the OHL. If you were a soft team, you had no hope. You didn't want the big, so-called tough guys going to Oshawa or something. The tough guys were at a premium. As you moved forward in time, you start to realize the importance of skill, and then some of the rules that came into the league changed things a bit. But there was probably an overemphasis on size and toughness in the early eighties, certainly compared to the way it is now."

On the road, behind the bench and in the room as the Petes trainer, Twohey was almost getting a paid apprenticeship. He was soaking in all he could from Dick Todd. He was spending a ton of time with Jacques Martin. He knew the legendary Roger Neilson, whose hockey school he used to work at. Throughout this time, Twohey was developing his own philosophy on the game. He was learning what the Petes were looking for. The lessons Twohey got from working at Neilson's hockey school were simple but important ones.

"The biggest thing I learned from Roger was 'Simplify the game.' I always had an idea that the game was complicated, but I would watch Roger and how he taught. I would work on videos with him. I would realize, 'It's not that complicated. I get it!' Roger simplified things. But most importantly, I learned how to treat people. Roger cared for people. If you wanted to learn about hockey, Roger would share. He was never protective of any information. I was around him a lot for a long period of time."

As for what the Petes were looking for? "We really cared about character. We wanted high-character guys that were good students. Roger was a pioneer in Peterborough, [with] the ability to combine school and hockey. If your skill level was limited, but you were a competitive guy with high character, we valued you."

And that's what led the Petes to draft Ross Wilson out of Sudbury with the fifteenth-overall pick in the 1986 OHL draft.

"Ross was a big winger who played for the Sudbury midgets," said Twohey. "I was sitting at the draft table, and I was adamant that he was the guy. There was some disagreement among the other scouts. I give Dick Todd credit; he gave me an opportunity. We took Ross in the first round."

Twohey got his guy, a big character kid out of Sudbury. It just took a bit of time for the kid Twohey had scouted to show his true form. "When he first came to camp, he struggled right off the bat. I thought, *My career is over,* but as the season progressed, he became a really valuable guy, to the point that, when he was nineteen, he had close to fifty goals. He was tough. He would play hard. He turned out to be a great pick. I didn't know it was going to be that good, but it worked out well.

"You do get some satisfaction out of it [when the team takes your guy]. We started to see that Ross was helping us win. It was a very unselfish group that we had in Peterborough. There was a commitment to winning. That's what was important. You could see Ross's high character. He fit in. The guys loved him. We could play Oshawa or Belleville and it didn't matter. He had no fear. He was a good player. There was a bit of relief that I made the right selection, but more so the fact that he could help us win."

He did, indeed. Ross Wilson was second in team scoring and won an OHL championship on the 1988–89 Petes, along with Mike Ricci and Tie Domi.

Eventually, Twohey lost the trainer title and was promoted to assistant coach and assistant GM. He was still scouting. As the years went on, Twohey developed another weapon for his scouting tool belt, one that can often be overlooked, especially in the hockey world. "I've always preached open-mindedness. You have to be open-minded."

You've heard the expression "One man's junk is another man's treasure." It applies in hockey, too. One night, Twohey was scouting a midget tournament. He wanted to check out the final game of the day, but first he had to sit through a game he didn't really want to check out. He was watching the game and not thinking much of it. "The game was almost putting me to sleep. As far as I could see, there were no prospects there."

A team from Montreal was having its way with a team from Oshawa. It wasn't even close. The blowout was on when a kid on the Montreal team ran Oshawa's goalie and then challenged the Oshawa bench. "And then I saw this kid on Oshawa grab him and just beat the crap out of him."

Twohey turned to a lady sitting beside him in the stands. "'That kid looks like he knows what he's doing.' The lady looked at me and said, 'He's never been beat.' The lady was the Oshawa player's mom." Twohey got the player's name. He had been passed over twice in the OHL draft. He had been cut from Tier II junior teams. Twohey put his name on the draft list anyway. Fast-forward to the 1995 OHL draft, and the Petes are mulling over their next selection, the 145th overall.

"I said to the scouts, 'I saw this guy. There is something about him. I'm just going take a chance.'"

The kid who looked like he knew what he doing just happened to be at the draft. He was waiting for it to come to an end. Shawn Thornton's plan was to sit around all day, and when the selections were done, he would sign a tryout agreement with the London Knights. Twohey had other plans. He selected Thornton. Thornton, a future Stanley Cup champion, was just as shocked as anyone when he heard his name called.

"I was in the bathroom when I heard," said Thornton. "I walked out. I saw that it was my name on the board. I even checked the program to make sure there weren't two Shawn Thorntons listed. I didn't know I was getting drafted. Jeff definitely didn't know I was going to be there because when I showed up at the Petes' table fifteen or twenty minutes later, they were shocked to see that I was in attendance."

Thornton's plans changed just like that. As a walk-on, he would have been a long shot to make the London Knights. He was going to give it a try, but he figured he would have ended up playing Junior B and then eventually trying to catch on with a Canadian college team. Instead, drafted by the Petes GM, he set his sights on gaining a spot on an OHL roster.

"The fact that Jeff was also the GM and found me, probably knowing hockey circles, that probably had a little bit of an impact [on my chances of making the Petes], too, other than some random scout. I'm not taking away from scouts, by the way, but having a GM see you and draft you probably has more of an impact than an every-day scout who has to prove his story to the GM."

The Petes told Thornton, an eighteen-year-old kid who'd played defence for most of his career, that they needed a fourth-line right winger who could stick up for himself and his teammates. He knew what to do when camp opened.

"First shift, I walked on the ice. The tough guy in Peterborough at the time was Johnny 'Boom Boom' Shamoon. He had made a name for himself in the OHL with the Petes, fighting some pretty tough guys the year before I got there. We had a good fight, and I guess they decided maybe I was a little bit better of a hockey player, and I ended up getting the job."

Shawn Thornton was part of the 1995–96 Petes team that hosted the Memorial Cup. A year later, in June of 1997, Thornton was drafted by the Toronto Maple Leafs in the seventh round, 190th overall. He played in 705 NHL regular-season games and won two Stanley Cups—not bad for a kid who just hoped to play Canadian college hockey.

"I had no aspirations of the NHL," he says. "I've said thank you to Jeff a million times. I don't get that opportunity without him."

What makes a good scout to Jeff Twohey?

"A big part of it is your instincts and being able to identify players. But I think it's also open-mindedness. Too often in this business, minds get closed. People say, 'Oh, this guy is eighteen. If he was any good, somebody else would have given him a chance.' Being open-minded is a big part of it."

For instance? Another player on the 1995–96 Petes was a once-upon-a-time gangly goalie.

"Do you remember Zac Bierk?" begins Twohey, who by 1995–96 was in his third season as Peterborough's general manager, a nice jump from trainer. "Zac played at Trinity College. Nobody knew about him. I had kind of heard about him. He had a family history. I went and watched him, and I froze my ass off. I thought, *Here's this big guy. He's really clumsy, but there's something there.* I phoned his mother and said we'd like to bring him to camp in the spring if he's interested."

Bierk was good enough to make it to Peterborough's main camp. He didn't exactly wow the brass. "I have to admit, he was awful. The scouting staff, the coaches and pretty much everybody said to me, 'Get rid of this guy.' The board of directors of the Petes said the same thing. I kept him. Three years later, we were in the Memorial Cup. He was overage player of the year."

What did Twohey see in this Bierk kid? Talent ran in his family, so Twohey figured the kid must be loaded with talent, too. Zac Bierk's father is David Bierk, an internationally known Canadian painter. *The National Post,* in an April 15, 2002, article, stated that "David Bierk is an artist whose work hangs everywhere from the collections of singer Sarah McLachlan to Hong Kong's Grand Hyatt Hotel." Zac's sister was a runway model. And his brother is Sebastian Bach, the rock star and former lead singer of Skid Row. So, Bierk came from an extremely successful family, but that didn't mean that any on-ice success was guaranteed. Twohey had to be patient; really patient.

"I really did not know. He had athletic ability, but he also was really raw. It goes back to being open-minded. As I always said, I look like a genius, but I'm not that smart. [Bierk] took the opportunity and ran with it. Scouting sometimes is looking at the big picture, not just the small picture. I saw an athletic kid, but more importantly than that, he came from a high-achieving family.

"When I signed Zac Bierk, I was laughing," Twohey continued. "I said, 'Berkey, someday we're going to be in the Memorial Cup and your brother is going to sing the national anthem.' Two years later, it happened. Really. Sebastian sang the anthem in Peterborough. There's a giant painting of Queen Elizabeth II that Bierk's father had done, and Sebastian was singing the national anthem, facing the painting that his father had done, and his brother was the starting goalie in the Memorial Cup. After we won that game, I ran into Sebastian. He put me in a headlock and kissed me."

Zac Bierk went on to play in forty-seven games with three different teams in the NHL. He is now the goalie coach of the Ottawa Senators.

Sometimes, it's the small things you say. When Twohey was in Peterborough, he was dealing with young men—or, as some people would call hockey players between the ages of sixteen and twenty, kids. Words matter, even when you don't think they do. Often, the simplest advice, even from a time when Twohey was a trainer/scout, could have a big impact.

"It was my very first year," says Rob Murray, the head coach of the Tulsa Oilers of the ECHL. "It was my very first exhibition game. We were playing at Chesswood Arena in Toronto against the Marlies. Coming out of midget, I had never fought. I was always a tough player, but I'd never actually had a hockey fight. I took on a guy named Jeff Cornelius, who was a veteran guy with the Marlies at the time. He hit me with an uppercut and split my lip."

Murray had to make his way with Jeff to the Petes' dressing room for repairs. Now, remember, Jeff didn't do stitches; he wasn't going to help Rob by fixing his lip, but he was going to help him with the mind game, which is often hockey's toughest battle. "Jeff just looked at me and said, 'You'll get him next time.' I was a fifteenth-round pick. I was just happy to be there. I didn't know whether I had a chance or not to make the team. I was just going to work every day; I did everything the coaches asked for, so I made the team. Later on that season, in Peterborough one night, sure enough, I found Jeff Cornelius again. I don't know if I can honestly say I beat the shit out of him or anything like that, but I can say I did very well. And I remember Jeff and me laughing about it and Jeff saying, 'I told you.'"

"Rob was a scrawny little centre that was mean, really mean. He was probably meaner than [former Pete] Chris Pronger," says Jeff. "Rob called me up one time when he was back in Peterborough. He said, 'Hey, I'm just going to drop over.' He came over. We were having a barbecue. We were having a beer. He said, 'Do you remember what you said to me when I was getting the shit beat out of me all the time when I was trying to make the team?'"

Twohey didn't remember. But Rob Murray did. He reminded Twohey of what those simple words meant to him. They were the words a fifteenth-round pick needed to hear. "Rob said from that moment on, he had no fear. My oldest daughter is a high school teacher, and I tell her, 'Never underestimate what you say to kids.' I said that to Rob Murray, not even thinking about it. I was just trying to encourage him. He set the all-time penalty minutes record in the American League."

That record has since been broken, but it was Murray's for a while. The fifteenth-round pick of the Petes in 1984 played pro for over a decade and a half. He scored four goals and added fifteen assists in 107 career NHL games for Washington, Winnipeg and Phoenix. He has been a professional coach since he retired in 2003. His number 23 is retired by Springfield of the American Hockey League. "His mentorship at times really allowed me to become the player I was at the time and to allow me to have success, to get drafted, to move on, to make a career out of this. My first training started with Jeff and Peterborough," says Murray.

"Jeff and I developed a very close relationship through the years. I think he respected the way I played. I knew that he was really in my corner, and that meant a whole lot to me, and it still does to this day. Through the years, we've kept in touch. We see each other on occasion, a little less now than ever, but we are always talking. I run names by him, guys that I'm trying to recruit that he may have seen. With the job I have here in Tulsa as an ECHL coach, you are tasked with finding the team, finding the players. A guy like Jeff is invaluable for that kind of information."

Twohey's junior days are behind him. He was with the Petes for three decades. He went on to scout for the Arizona Coyotes, with a couple of OHL stops in between. He is now an amateur scout for the Florida Panthers.

"I used to think when I was in junior that the NHL scouting was easy because in most cases, it's just one game a day, whereas in junior you could be watching a tournament that is ten or twelve games. But when you get into it, you start to realize maybe how little you know about how to organize your schedule. There are specific things you have to do at the NHL level when you fill out your reports. There are background things you have to do. The basics of identifying players remains the same, but there's a lot more work that goes into it behind the scenes. You need to understand what the team's philosophy is. When I was in junior, players had to fit into my philosophy because I was the general manager," said Twohey. "Now I work for other people. There are certain standards that they have. You have to understand what the general manager values. There is a lot more organization that goes into it because of travel. When I scouted for the Coyotes, for instance, I was covering the world. You had to figure out when to go to Finland or when to go to the Czech Republic. You had to go wherever the players were, whereas as in junior, you were just kind of in Ontario."

In other words, no more hitchhiking.

CHAPTER 9

The Singing Scout

Bill Heffernan

Bill Heffernan has worn many hats over the years—factory worker, musician and hockey scout. COURTESY PAUL PATSKOU

With his guitar strapped over his shoulder, Bill Heffernan was weaving a tale as he prepared to play a song. Heffernan looks every bit the singer that he is. With a white beard and long hair tucked under his black sailor cap, he looks like the kind of folksinger you would find on the East Coast of Canada. That makes sense. After all, Heffernan's birth mother was from Cape Breton.

Growing up in a life of poverty, she gave up her young son for adoption. Heffernan grew up in Etobicoke, Ontario, not far from where he is weaving his way through his story on this day at the Scotiabank Pond in Toronto. It's a modern hockey rink with four sheets of ice. And on the first Monday of each month, the restaurant at the Pond plays host to an NHL Alumni Lunch put on by hockey historian Paul Patskou, and you never know who might show up. On this day, if you looked around the crowd, you could see former Leafs general manager Gerry McNamara, Hockey Hall of Fame writer Scott Morrison and a former Leafs goalie, the great Mike Palmateer. And right now, those three, and everyone else in the room, were glued to the tale Heffernan was telling.

"The hockey scouts would often carpool," began Heffernan, recalling his days as a scout for the Winnipeg Jets in the 1980s. "You see, we were all getting paid mileage, and if you put five scouts in a car, you only had to fill up one car's worth of gas. And then we'd all bill our clubs the mileage. I think we were green before anybody was green."

Heffernan was talking about the time he and a gaggle of scouts took in a Saturday afternoon Toronto Marlboros game at Maple Leaf Gardens years ago. The luxury of an afternoon game in Toronto meant that if you got out of town soon enough, you could catch another game that night somewhere down the highway. On this particular Saturday, there was a game that night in Belleville. So, Heffernan did what he always did. He hopped in a car with four other scouts. Heffernan, being the youngest, got the middle seat in the back. There were two scouts riding up front and three in the back. To Heffernan's left was another scout. To his right, though, was not just a scout.

"I had the worst seat in the car every time, but I was so thankful that I got the hump seat this day because on my right was the legendary Glenn Hall."

As in Mr. Goalie. He was a Stanley Cup champion and the holder of perhaps hockey's most unbreakable record: Hall played 502 consecutive complete games.

The Hockey Hall of Famer was on a scouting trip for the Calgary Flames, and at this moment was in the back seat of the same car as Bill Heffernan and doing the same thing, heading down Highway 401 to Belleville, Ontario, to see the Bulls play at the Quinte Sports Centre.

"As we left Maple Leaf Gardens and got up on the 401, the two scouts in the front started peppering Glenn Hall with questions," Heffernan told the crowd. "Glenn went silent. He never said a word. He wasn't interested in the scouts' questions. The guy on my left asked a question, too. And then he figured it out. Glenn stayed silent. He was as quiet as he could be, and he was looking out the window just as we passed Oshawa."

Then, in a clearing by the side of the 401, Hall spotted a flock of geese. He stayed silent as he watched the geese cross the sky. Heffernan, ever the artist, stayed silent, too. He never asked Hall a question. Heffernan knew, though, that he had to do something. "As a songwriter, I had to write this song. It's called 'Glenn and the Geese.'"

With the crowd of fifty or sixty old-school hockey fans hanging on his every word, Heffernan finally strummed his guitar. He sang his song about a road trip with the greatest goalie of all time. A goalie who said more in his silence than his words ever could.

Once Heffernan strummed the final note, the room erupted. Hockey fans, won over by a song about a legend, a quiet legend, on a scouting trip with Bill Heffernan and a few others on the 401 so many years ago.

"What did I learn from Glenn's silence on that drive?" Heffernan pondered about an hour after leaving the stage. "Glenn was a man who worked on a farm. He's a classic working-class guy. He's an old farmer. I think what he could accomplish as an athlete was admirable, but in many ways, I think he would have been just as good of a truck driver or a farmer. So, all these years later, all the questions he was being asked meant nothing to him. I was intrigued by him and the geese. When I finally contacted Glenn, he said, 'You know, thank you for writing the song. You got it right!' He said he really cares about the environment. So, Glenn was a guy who lives in the moment. That's what I learned."

Bill Heffernan learned to live in the moment as a songwriter, too. Much like Glenn Hall, he lives, and writes, for the moment. "I mean, I do some old hit songs to keep people happy, but the main thing is to keep moving on. Keep progressing, be where you are, live in the moment. I think Glenn Hall did that. He was not interested in being this old guy to all these people. So, as soon as I saw that on the drive, I didn't ask any questions."

Bill Heffernan the singer was once—and is once again—Bill Heffernan the hockey scout. But he has also been Bill Heffernan the guidance counsellor and Bill Heffernan the factory worker. He has worn a lot of hats. He has lived in a lot of moments. He has learned a lot of lessons in his seventy-three years. The lasting one, though, he conveys to the crowd at this alumni lunch. With the event's onstage host, Andrew Applebaum, to his right, he told another tale from the stage.

Heffernan reached all the way back to his hockey-obsessed life as a child in Etobicoke. "I played Knights of Columbus hockey because we were Catholic. I scored buckets of goals in elementary school. I played every sport possible. So, when I got to high school, I figured I'm a cinch to make the Michael Power [High School] hockey team. Good hockey players came out of Michael Power. I went to the tryouts with my neighbour Jimmy. I knew Jimmy couldn't play. I knew he was going to get cut. After the tryout, we looked at the list and I got cut. My hockey-playing career was over one month before I turned fourteen—at least competitive hockey—but somehow by age thirty or thirty-one, I ended up in the NHL."

That "somehow" started right away for young Bill Heffernan. He couldn't believe he had been cut, but he immediately made a plan.

It was five fifteen on a November afternoon and it was getting dark. Bill asked Jimmy to take his gear home for him. "I need you to carry my hockey bag because if I run out the back door of the arena, and if I hop across the creek and get up on the railway trestle, the one that our parents had warned us to never cross—that railway trestle, the one where kids actually got killed . . . if I get through the trestle and hop over the fence into the seminary, I know there's a little gate and I can cut through to the Michael Power gym's back door by five thirty and I can try out for the bantam basketball team."

Young Bill Heffernan did just that. Jimmy grabbed his equipment and Bill bolted. Out the back door. Across the trestle. Into the seminary. Through the gate and the back door of the gym. He made the basketball team, too. "I played five years of basketball and five years of football. And that railway trestle is the motif of my life. When one door closes, another might open!" Bill says proudly.

Heffernan's athletic career, like those of pretty much everyone on the planet, ended after high school. He went to university, dropped out and got a job in a factory. One day, he and a buddy, Johnny O'Flaherty, went to the track. Johnny's brother Billy was there. Bill Heffernan didn't know Billy O'Flaherty too well. O'Flaherty had been away for the past few years, playing hockey at Clarkson College in Potsdam, New York. With his playing career all wrapped up, O'Flaherty was now back in Toronto.

Bill and Billy hit it off. Eventually, Billy O'Flaherty started working as an assistant coach with Clarkson. That meant he would scout games in the Toronto area. Bill Heffernan started to tag along to the games with his pal. Eventually, though, Billy O'Flaherty would have to venture out of Toronto on scouting trips. He would be off to Montreal one week and Saskatchewan the next. He needed someone to keep an eye on the prospects around Toronto. "He asked me, 'Can you keep an eye on this kid or that kid?' That's how my scouting started."

It didn't take long for Heffernan to find his groove. "I found a kid that no one else had found out of Malton Arena," said Heffernan. "He was older and he only played one year of Junior B. I convinced Clarkson to take him, and he became an All-American. He centred the great Dave Taylor, who went to play on the Triple Crown Line. My first two picks to go to Clarkson became very good players. I had a lot of trust from the head coach at Clarkson, Jerry York, and Bill O'Flaherty."

Just like that, Bill Heffernan was a scout. He and Johnny O'Flaherty would go to games all over Toronto to look for the next great Clarkson star. The scouting eventually led to a coaching job for Bill with the Royal York Royals of the Ontario Provincial Junior Hockey League. It was a Tier II league; in other words, a fair share of the players in the league were out to win NCAA scholarships. Eighty players showed up for tryouts, Bill's first as part of a Junior A coaching staff. "So, I'm watching eighty guys on the ice. I sat by myself for the first seven minutes, and I made the classic mistake. I looked for the best player. And then I looked for the next best player. And after four or five minutes, I realized, 'We got to cut forty guys! I'm doing this wrong! I'm going to look for the worst player.'"

After the two-hour session, Bill and the rest of the coaches, staff and owners had a meeting. How were they going to cut forty guys? Someone suggested looking at the players' bios and making cuts based on where they had played the previous year. Did they play AAA or AA? That would make it easier. Bill was not buying into that plan.

"I said, 'Well, you can do that, or how would you like to know the worst forty players on the ice, and we cut them?'"

The staff agreed to Bill's proposal. "We kept following that procedure. The best players will always be the best. You don't need to identify them in training camp. You got to make sure that your twenty-first player is better than your twenty-second."

A young kid who had played AA the year before kept surviving the cuts. He made it to the very end of training camp. It was time for a decision, though. Were the Royal York Royals going to cut the young kid who'd played AA in Etobicoke the year before, or were they going to cut a kid out of AAA who had been chosen by Kingston in the OHL draft? It was a tough call. The players had been pretty much equal through camp. The rest of the men in charge of the Royal York Royals wanted to keep the drafted kid. Bill Heffernan wanted to stick with the young guy out of AA.

"I said, 'You're telling me that they're tied! They're even! The AA kid didn't play anywhere! He's going to be way ahead of this AAA guy in another year.'"

Bill got his way. The Royals kept the AA kid. He was a defenceman named Bruce Driver. The sixteen-year-old defenceman scored forty-two points in forty-nine games in his first year with the Royals. He had seventy points in his second year. Then he went and played three years at the University of Wisconsin, where he won two NCAA championships, including one in his final year with the Badgers, when he was captain of the team. After leaving Wisconsin, he played for Canada at the 1984 Olympics. Driver had 486 points in 922 NHL games with the New Jersey Devils and New York Rangers. He won a Stanley Cup with the Devils in 1995. That's not bad for a kid who was almost the last cut of the Royal York Royals. "I think I was a little unorthodox, but I was looking for players that may have been overlooked but were progressing."

"Absolutely, oh absolutely," says Bruce Driver when he is asked about a guy like Bill, and how he helped make a difference in his journey when major junior teams weren't exactly knocking down his doors. "Bill Heffernan was a big part of that, and my head coach, Ken Gibb, was a big part of that as well. For me, I remember those years."

Those years with the Royal York Royals led to the next step in the journey for Driver—a scholarship to Wisconsin. "It was the best move for me. I was more or less just going there because they were going to pay for my education. But it really changed things for me. If I didn't go there, I probably wouldn't be talking to you today about an NHL career."

Future Stanley Cup champion Colin Patterson led the Royals in scoring one year. Bill ended up getting Patterson to Clarkson. Other players went to other schools, some more quickly than others. One season, the Royals had the rights to a young scorer named Rick Kuraly. He was lighting it up with a local juvenile team, scoring four or five goals a night. "He was just too good for that league, but he was undisciplined because he could do what he wanted. He was buried in juvenile. He was not a great skater, but he had a long, long stride and if he ever got his skating straightened out, this guy could be something," Bill recalls.

One night, Kuraly got his chance. Half an hour before a game was set to start, the Royals captain told the coaches he was too sick to play. The team put in the call for Rick Kuraly. The head coach wanted to shuffle up the lines. Heffernan disagreed. He told the head coach to just insert Kuraly into the captain's spot on the first line. Heffernan figured Kuraly was a goal scorer, so he would fit in nicely on the top unit. Kuraly arrived at the rink in time. He met up with Heffernan. "I said, 'Rick, you've got one job tonight. I don't want you even trying to score. I want you to stay on your wing all night long, up and down, up and down, up and down. Don't leave the wing all night.'"

Heffernan made his way out of the dressing room. He then ran into a scout he had never seen before. He was from an American college that was going to start up a Division I program the next season—Miami University in Ohio. The scout told Heffernan he was impressed with his team. "You got a wagon." But he said he couldn't compete with the big schools for the top players. Heffernan gave the scout a list of the twelve players on the Royals who were NCAA-eligible. "He comes to me at the end of the night, and he says, 'You know, there's one guy on your team that really intrigued me. He was the most disciplined player on your team.' It was Rick Kuraly," Heffernan chuckles.

That stay-on-your-wing advice paid off. Heffernan's plan was to have Kuraly play for the Royals the next season and then send him on his way to Clarkson. Instead, the juvenile call-up was immediately offered a scholarship to Miami of Ohio. "They took him after one game! He scored [101 goals in college], and I thought he went a year too early. Rick Kuraly—it's those kinds of stories I love. He got an education. He had a great career. His son played for the US junior development team [Sean, who went on to the NHL as well]. Rick married an American girl, stayed in Dublin, Ohio. It's those kind of scouting stories, for me, that are a delight."

"That's what life is. You get an opportunity and try and make the most of it," says Kuraly, who still holds the Miami of Ohio record for career goals, with 101.

"I don't know how to explain it. Bill was just very direct and concentrated. He knew what he was talking about and he could explain it in a few words. It wasn't long stories or anything like that. I don't know if it's still the same way; we're talking about forty years ago now. Bill was very well respected. You tried to play well for him."

And then there are the superstars. While he was scouting and coaching, Bill also began a career in education. He eventually moved on to the OHL for a brief stint with the Sudbury Wolves before joining the NHL as a part-time scout for the Winnipeg Jets. One night, Bill got a call from an old friend, Ken Gibb, the head coach back when Bill was an assistant coach with the Royals. Gibb was now the head coach of the Markham Waxers of the Ontario Junior Hockey League, and he had a problem. "He said, 'Billy, I've got a player that's better than anyone I've ever seen, but no colleges are coming to the games.' I said, 'Well, Gibber, what's his name?' He told me his name. I said, 'I got a note on that guy.'"

Bill had kept all his notes from his scouting adventures. He knew the player right away. "I said, 'He's really smart, he's crafty, really good—small, but he's a really good centre.'"

Gibb told Billy the player was not small anymore. So, what was the problem? Bill asked what grade the player was in. He was met with silence. It turned out the player was not in school at all. He had dropped out. "I go, 'Gibber, no one is going to come and give him a scholarship. He doesn't even have his Grade 12.' I said, 'Send that kid to my office. I want to talk to him about school.'"

Gibb got a hold of the player. This uber-talented player, along with his father, his coach and the commissioner of the league met with Bill Heffernan. The problem for the player was that he had played one or two exhibition games with the major junior Toronto Marlboros. That made him ineligible for the NCAA. And he was buried on the Waxers. The Marlies were loaded with top-end centres, so this kid was not going to get his chance with the Marlies. He was buried in Markham. Bill Heffernan had a plan, though. "Under NCAA rules, if the player didn't know he was making himself ineligible by playing in an exhibition game, there was a provision which I knew about. You could appeal to play NCAA hockey, but you would have to sit out the first semester. But if you won your appeal, then you could play the rest of your career."

Bill Heffernan told the kid to go back to school right away and finish the twelfth grade. The player did exactly that. He continued to light it up on the ice, too. Bill was right: The player was eventually deemed eligible to play NCAA hockey. That kid, named Adam Oates, made the dean's list at Rensselaer Polytechnic Institute. Oates scored ninety-one points in thirty-eight games in his final season and capped his college career off with an NCAA title. He is a Hockey Hall of Famer who put up a stunning 1,420 regular-season points in his NHL career.

Heffernan continued to scout for the Winnipeg Jets throughout the 1980s. He was very content with where he fit in. The Jets wanted him to keep an eye out for anyone flying under the radar, which was more than fine with him. "The only reason Winnipeg hired me was that I had a beat on the Tier II and Junior B late developers. They wanted to get kids in college. It was mostly American, but I'm going to give you a name of a fabulous goal scorer that we got in Winnipeg out of college hockey in Canada: Paul MacLean. And he went on to coach the Ottawa Senators. We believed that there were diamonds in the rough."

The Jets were led off the ice by the front-office trio of John Ferguson, Mike Doran and Mike Smith.

"It was clear that underneath the big three, my opinion was as valued as anybody else's. They wanted me to go full time. The only difference between a part-time scout and a full-time scout is the pay. You have to go to games every night, and I was happy as a part-time scout. The Jets gave me a lot of leeway."

At the same time as he was scouting, Heffernan was also working in education. Approaching his fortieth birthday, he was offered to take over as the head of the guidance department at the school he worked at in Brampton, Ontario.

"When I was teaching, I was getting away with going to games every night and going to school every day. On any weekend, I could've been in Ohio, I could've been in Massachusetts, I could've been in Quebec, I could've been anywhere in Ontario. I loved it, but you can't keep doing that. It had to be one of the other, so I chose the teaching."

And that closed the book on Bill Heffernan's scouting career—for the next thirty years. But now he is back.

He ran into his former head coach at Clarkson, Jerry York, at York's Hockey Hall of Fame induction. That got Heffernan thinking. A few other run-ins got him thinking more. Then one night, an old scouting buddy, Paul Henry, stopped by his house. As Henry got up to leave, Heffernan asked where he was going. Henry, of course, was off to a game, a Junior A game in Collingwood. Something inside of

Heffernan made him move. He jumped in with Henry and headed to the game. Soon enough, Bill saw a kid he really liked. Forty-eight hours later, he was back to watch him again. "I went back two nights later on my own to see if I was dreaming or not. And then I found another guy. But I've been out of the business thirty years! What am I going to with this information? So, I told Clarkson about these two kids that I'd seen."

Clarkson didn't get the kids. But Niagara University did. They both got scholarships. And now, for the first time in over three decades, Bill Heffernan is scouting again. He's doing it pro bono for Clarkson for the time being, but like any good adventure, he's going to see where it takes him. "One of the Clarkson coaches is thirty-four years old and I'm thirty-five years out of the game! Who am I? It's going take a while, but I got the bug.

"It's very interesting because since I have returned, I have learned that the art of scouting, the rigour of scouting, the doing of scouting, individually scouting a player, has not changed. I found no real change. In fact, I was surprised how quickly I was right back into it."

However, the game has changed unbelievably, in Heffernan's view. "What coaches are looking for and may want from their scouts could be different. I made my bread and butter by being honest, straightforward, and reporting what I saw. I never hang around with any other scouts until intermission or travel to this day. I can't believe how many scouts go to a game and sit with each other. I think that produces—not always, but there is a danger that it can produce—group think. And the other danger is you start talking to the guy beside you, you know, maybe there's a shift where there's no one out there that you're watching. I always sat by myself. And I'm an extremely social person, but I sat by myself. You're never as good as your past. You're only where you are in the moment."

Like picking up a guitar and singing a song, scouting is something that comes pretty naturally to Bill Heffernan. The two vocations, though, couldn't be further apart. When you're a singer, you're the one in the spotlight, at centre stage. When you're a scout, you're in the background, watching the performer. Has Bill ever thought of the juxtaposition of the two things he does best—scouting and singing?

"No, I haven't thought about that," he ponders. "I told you I was adopted at birth. My two mothers couldn't have been more different. The answer to that question is my two mothers. When I'm on stage, that's the only place I want to be. When I'm scouting, on my own, that's the only place I want to be."

CHAPTER 10

An Island of Opportunities

Shane Turner

Shane Turner (right) at the 2020 Bridgestone Winter Classic with his sons Dustin (left) and fellow hockey scout Brett. COURTESY SHANE TURNER

Shane Turner, in his mid-sixties, doesn't have to spend his winter nights on the icy roads of Quebec and Atlantic Canada, but he does. Turner doesn't have to spend his winter nights in cold rinks, but he does. He doesn't have to spend his spare time in coffee shops from Newfoundland to Quebec, but he does. He doesn't have to take up a Monday filing paperwork on his latest scouting adventure, but yes, he does.

"People say get a passion for something. I don't think you can just say, 'Okay, I'm going to do this and I'm going get a passion for it.' I think you have to like something, and then you start doing it a lot, and I think the passion develops from that. I think that's what happened with me and scouting," says Turner, a long-time Dallas Stars scout.

Turner does not need to scout, but he does, because he loves it. The business world treated Shane Turner, born and bred in Charlottetown, PEI, very well. He worked in the oil and gas business for both Irving and Shell. He ended up owning a Junior A team in Charlottetown, the Abbies, and was part of an ownership group with the American Hockey League's PEI Senators in the mid-1990s. By now, he could be putting his feet up on a beach in Florida; instead, he keeps his head up, and his feet in the stands, looking for that next great hockey find.

"I love it. I absolutely love it. The travel is starting to beat me up, I have to be honest. But I love being in the rinks."

Shane Turner never planned on ending up in the scouting business. He never even planned on a life in hockey. He was just a kid who loved the game.

It's a classic story. His old man worked two jobs and would flood the backyard rink during the winter. Soon enough, Shane was playing organized hockey in Charlottetown. There was a difference between Turner and the other kids, though. He was really good. Good enough to skip midget hockey and, at the age of fourteen, play for Forbes Kennedy, one of the toughest to ever lace them up and a PEI legend. The one-time NHLer made the pitch to Mr. and Mrs. Turner for their young son to join his Junior A team in the mid-1970s. It was a hell of a jump for a kid who would now be playing against twenty-year-old men. "Forbes went to my folks and said, 'I know what age Shane is, but don't you worry, I will take care of him.' And he did."

Kennedy wasn't he only one taking care of the fourteen-year-old in the mean world of PEI junior hockey in the 1970s. Of course he had a teammate or two to look out for him, including a guy named Paul Arsenault. Arsenault took more than just one punch to the face for his fourteen-year-old teammate. "His nose is all over his face, but he's still a really good friend today."

Shane didn't have to worry about *his* nose being splattered all over his face. His nose was for the net. That was true from the start: he scored two goals in his first-ever Junior A game. How young was he? Well, his head coach, Kennedy, drove him home after that first game. Kennedy gave Turner some simple advice that night. It was simple, but it stuck because it was to the point, and it has worked for all these years. "It was, 'Yeah, you got two goals tonight, but that's just the start of the journey. It's really all about how hard you work and being a good teammate.' It was really cool. It didn't mean more until I was older, obviously."

As he got older, Turner briefly explored the hockey wilderness off his island. He had a tryout with the Montreal Bleu Blanc Rouge. The team wanted to keep him around on another junior team in the Montreal area, but his dad told him to come home and focus on his education. So, Turner did. He enrolled at the University of Prince

Edward Island and joined the school's hockey team, the Panthers. By his third season, he was third on the team in points. One night, his coach told him there were some guys coming to watch him play. That's when Shane Turner actually began to think he could have a future in the game.

"I never even thought of pro. I just enjoyed playing. I enjoyed getting to the rink. I don't recall who those guys who came to watch me were, but our coach was also a scout for the New York Islanders. And that's where I ended up going because of that connection."

If it sounds kind of simple, that's because it was—and it wasn't. Turner, a speedy, undersized forward, spent a lot of time playing hockey, but he didn't spend a of time fantasizing about a life in the pros. It just happened. He spent the summer of 1980 training, 1980-style. "In hindsight, everything I did was probably wrong. I had no one to train me. I just did whatever I read in a book. I was doing bench presses every day and all this stuff. I wasn't doing the right things, but anyway, I had fun. I enjoyed it."

Soon enough, the five-foot, nine-inch Turner was off to try and crack the roster of the defending Stanley Cup champs. Despite his rudimentary training regimen, he was actually in good shape. "I did really well in training camp. I was one of the leading scorers, if not the leading point getters, and I thought that was really good. But in hindsight in later years, I looked back at the Bossys playing two games, the Trottiers, Nystrom one or two, and I was playing all of them," he laughs.

The Islanders were a stacked bunch. There was no way Turner was going to make the team, but he learned what made hockey players tick at that level. There were things that did not show up on a stat sheet, or even on the ice. "Bryan Trottier sat down with me. I'm sure he doesn't remember it. It was one day in training camp. We had a great conversation. I really appreciated it. Another day, I stayed on after practice. I asked Bob Nystrom to help me with board play because I knew that was my weakest spot. I needed to work on it. Bob stayed on the ice with me and he worked with me. And he didn't have to do that. These guys were ensconced. They had just won their first Cup. They didn't have to help me.

"Another time," he continued, "Clark Gillies and Butch Goring took me and Kevin Devine, and a couple of others, four of us, and we went out to shoot some pool and just have a beer. Nothing serious. They just told us the experience of being on the team. They basically laid the groundwork for what you had to do if you wanted to become an Islander. 'This is the way we are.'"

Turner may not have known it at the time, but he was laying the groundwork for his future profession. The things he was seeing were the things he would look for in players one day. Who worked hard? Who worked on his weaknesses? Who was a good teammate? These things, aside from who simply dazzled on the ice, would help him in his still-far-off adventure as an NHL scout. "I like to go and see who works. Who gets along with their teammates in practice. Who is encouraging. Who is helping each other out. Are they on early? Do they stay on late?"

In the early 1980s, though, Turner wasn't the one doing the scouting; he was the one looking to impress the eyes high in the sky. He had a solid first pro season in 1980–81 with the Islanders' top farm team, the Indianapolis Checkers of the Central Hockey League. Turner had twenty-one points in seventy-one games. But, just thirteen games into his second season in Indianapolis, his pro career came to an end. He took a hip check on the knee one night. He didn't even have the puck at the time. Not surprisingly—these were the early 1980s, after all—sports science wasn't exactly up to snuff at the time. "I came back. It just wasn't the same. I couldn't cut one way—I didn't really know why. It just bothered me. It probably took away a lot of confidence from me.

"I just didn't feel that I was the same player. I just didn't have the confidence. When I finally went to a doctor, I didn't have an ACL. I didn't know. It really took an element of my game away because I was quick. I had really good edges. I could cut and swerve and get out of people's way, which was important for a guy my size."

And that was it for Shane Turner's pro career. He had chances to go to Europe, but stayed on PEI, went back to school and played some senior hockey. He eventually ended up winning a Hardy Cup, Canada's national intermediate championship, with the Charlottetown Islanders in 1984. While all this was happening, Turner ran into a rather influential Maritimer one night—unbeknownst to him.

"I met a gentleman and I had a long chat with him. He didn't know who I was. I actually didn't know who he was. At the end of it he said, 'I like your values and your perspective and where your head is. If you're ever looking for a job . . .' I said I had one year of university to finish, and I wanted to go back and get my degree and see what was ahead of me. Maybe I'd look at pro hockey again. After that, I'm not sure what I'm going to do. He said, 'That's fine, here's my card.'"

Turner didn't think much of it. He got home and told his dad about the chance encounter. His dad asked to see the business card. The name on the card was Robert Irving—as in the future co-CEO of the J. D. Irving conglomerate. Turner's dad told him to call Irving. He did. Turner finished his degree and worked for Irving at the same time. It started a lifetime in business for Turner. For the next several years, he stayed as close to the game as he could, playing, coaching and owning hockey teams. He would get asked from time to time if he'd like to scout, and he would decline.

One night in Calgary, though, it finally happened. Turner was at a Hockey Canada event. One of his roommates was long-time Peterborough Petes head coach Dick Todd, who would end up with the second-most coaching wins in Ontario Hockey League history. Turner and Todd would stay up late at night, doing what hockey people do—talking hockey. "So, it wasn't long after that Dick said to me, 'If you're ever looking for anything, give me a call.'"

So, Turner did. He told Todd he was not interested in leaving PEI. He had a business based on the island and didn't want to leave. Todd asked Turner if he would he like to scout. Soon enough, Turner was on the phone with Petes assistant GM Jeff Twohey, and the next few decades of his life were put into motion. "We had a conversation, and Jeff and I hit it off and we are still really good friends to this day. I stayed with them for them for seventeen years."

So, just like that, Turner, the ex-hockey player and now ex-coach, was a scout. At the start, there was a learning curve for the hockey lifer. "I looked at the game from a coach's perspective because I had been coaching for quite a few years by then, and that's the totally wrong way to look at it. Looking at the game from a coach's perspective is the here and now. Looking at it from a scouting perspective is where is this kid going to be in three to five years. Does he have the demeanour and work ethic to work on his game?"

Turner combed Atlantic Canada. A few of the kids he saw ended up with the Petes, sometimes ultimately reaching the NHL. Others walked other paths in life. There's Jonathan Murphy, a first-round pick of the Petes who is now a school principal in PEI. There's a guy like Billy McGuigan, a former OHL tough guy who has become a long-time Junior A coach in Summerside. There's Joey MacDonald, who went on to tend the twine in the NHL. And there's a guy like Kris MacPhee, a former junior speedster who is now a hockey mainstay on PEI. "What a great young man he is," says Turner. "He has his own fitness business now, and he works for Hockey PEI as well. The family has a meat business in North River. To this day, I still send all kinds of friends there to get their steaks."

"I think that I'm grateful when I hear the name Shane Turner," says MacPhee, a proud hockey dad of two daughters. "Back in 1997, 1998, it didn't seem like there were as many opportunities as there is now to play major junior. All of a sudden, I got a phone call from a guy by the name of Shane Turner. He was a scout for the Peterborough Petes. That was kind of the beginning of me having the opportunity of a lifetime, of having a dream of playing in the OHL come true. The number one thing I think of when I hear the name is being grateful for that opportunity. It was almost like a dream of ours that we could actually go to Ontario and play in the OHL. I remember watching Eric Lindros on a Sunday afternoon game . . . it was almost hard to believe that I could go there. So, when Shane calls and he is scouting for the Peterborough Petes, I was thinking, *Is this actually really happening?* Shane was a great guy. He still is today. He has had a big impact on guys from PEI, and he is still giving opportunities to guys now with scouting and other opportunities within the game."

Turner and the Petes won OHL championships. After seventeen seasons, Turner made the jump to the NHL with the Dallas Stars for the 2008–09 season. His outlook on scouting—most importantly, *who* he was scouting for—had to change. "Junior scouting is short term. You are going to have a player for probably two or three years—four max if you bring them in early. But generally, three years. In pro, you are looking at guys that, once you draft them, you can hand them off to your development staff and minor-pro coaches or their junior coaches. If they are still in junior, you work at getting these guys better. You are looking at probably three to five years from when you draft them to when you are getting them into the NHL. The NHL is a long-term approach. In pro, it is a different style than in junior. In junior, you are not always looking for who would be a nice bottom-six player. You are looking to get the best skill you can, and then you kind of fill in your roster."

The bottom-six player—the nugget. Finding that nugget is one of the main skills that any good amateur scout should have. Anyone can point out a Connor McDavid on the ice, but who can find that diamond in the rough? Who can find that under-the-radar guy who can make an unforeseen impact at the NHL level? Well, rarely does it happen alone. "With Dallas, it is very cooperative. We just want the best player. We don't care if he is from Russia, Finland, Sweden, North America—we don't care. We just want the best player. Our goal is to win now."

Sometimes, to win now, a hockey scout has to dig back a little bit. How do you find that missing piece? The hidden gems take a little more work to find.

After the 2011–12 season, the Stars were looking to strengthen up their AHL affiliate, the Texas Stars. The team wasn't looking for a superstar, just a guy who was tough to play against. Shane Turner and another Dallas scout thought of a kid named Antoine Roussel. "My fellow Dallas scout Alex Lepore and I, we always loved Antoine's ability to compete, his work ethic. And he could skate quickly in a straight line, but his mobility and agility needed work."

Roussel was nothing special on paper. He was never drafted into the QMJHL. He was never drafted into the NHL. He spent his first pro season in Boston's minor-league system—a healthy scratch in the AHL from time to time, with a little time in the ECHL mixed in as well. Turner had been keeping an eye on Roussel since his junior days, though. "I first saw him in the Quebec League, playing in

Chicoutimi," Turner says of Roussel. "He was just a hard-working guy. He didn't have a lot of skill like some of the other players, but I admired his work ethic and his compete and his drive. He just worked and worked and worked. He wasn't afraid of anybody. He was physical. He drove to the net. He had all the things you look for in those bottom-six attributes in a player."

Remember those things Shane Turner saw at New York Islanders camp back in 1980? Remember how Turner was the guy working on his weakness after a practice? Remember how he saw how well the veteran Islanders treated their rookies? Those are the qualities Turner saw in Antoine Roussel.

"My first year pro, Butch Cassidy was my assistant coach," says Roussel, who had one goal and eight assists in his first minor-league season. "I was bugging him a lot. I kept asking him, 'Hey, what should I do better?' He was exhausted of me asking him all this stuff. I was the first one at the rink every day. I was in the gym, doing extra work. I was the first one on the ice. I was the last one on the ice, doing all the little things that kept me around that first year."

Those little things kept Roussel around that first year, but they did not get him a contract. The Bruins let him go after his first year as a pro. He spent that summer back home in Quebec, skating with players like Pascal Dupuis and Alexandre Burrows, another one-time NHLer who started near the bottom of the pro ladder. "It was a big summer of training for me. Alex Burrows was so good to me."

Roussel was on the ice five times a week. He took the weekends off. That summer, he actually started calling scouts himself, leaving voice mails, asking, begging, for something, anything. He still remembers how the messages would go: "It's Antoine. I think I could be a big addition to your club, if I could just get an invite to your training camp or your rookie camp."

Persistence pays off. Roussel's play got him an invite to Vancouver's rookie camp. He made it to the main camp, lasted for most of it, but was eventually sent to the Chicago Wolves of the AHL. He did not go there with a frown on his face. "I got a contract with the Wolves. I felt pretty good about myself. Everything went so well at Canucks camp, but then I started to play a little less well, and then I hurt myself. I was thinking I still need to work on a few things, like puck protection, making plays. Fighting is good, but you stay in the league if you make plays."

Roussel was not working on the fancy stuff. But he was working on the things that could make him better—protecting the puck, moving the puck. These things don't show up on the score sheet, but maybe, just maybe the right people would notice. Roussel kept working. Yes, he would be scratched from time to time, kept out of the lineup, but he kept doing the things he felt he needed to do to stay at the AHL level and maybe earn an NHL contract. "I wasn't collecting points, but I was getting a few goals here and there. I remember having to battle for the fourth-line centre job with another guy on the Wolves. I think he was a second-round pick for Vancouver, but the good thing with the Wolves was the Wolves, they didn't care. They didn't give a damn if you were under contract with the Canucks. They played the player that they wanted to play. The coaching decisions are made by the Wolves, not by the Canucks."

That was a huge difference for Roussel. The Wolves were not being forced to play the Canucks' prospects. Unlike a lot of AHL teams, they could play the players they felt would help them win that night. "That was a huge help for me, to be on that team, at the end of the day. Even when I wasn't producing, I was making enough plays to stay in the lineup. I was a player that the other team didn't like [to play against], so the Wolves kept me in the lineup. If you look at my stats that year—yeah, they are shit," he continued. "Four goals and five assists in sixty-one games." But there was a *but*. And Roussel knew there was a *but*. Converted from a winger in junior to a centre in pro, he just needed to trust that someone was seeing the *but*. "If you watched the game, you would've said, 'Oh man, this guy is moving here. He's working hard.' I found a way by the end of that second year to be a centre. I loved playing centre. I found a way to be creative on the ice. I'm not saying that I was Wayne Gretzky out there, but I was making plays in the slot, creating scoring chances. I wanted to make one or two passes within the ten minutes of ice that I got per game to get into the slot, to create a screen chance for us, having a chance [at] being an inside player."

That's what Turner and the Dallas Stars saw, going all the way back to Roussel's junior days in Chicoutimi and now throughout his first two years as a pro. They saw the *but*. They saw the things you didn't see on a game sheet. Looking to shore up their AHL team, the Dallas Stars signed Roussel to a two-year, $1,225,000 contract on July 2, 2012. He did not have to spend the summers working the phones. He'd get the full cash if he played at the NHL level, but Roussel was destined for the AHL. He knew it and the Stars knew it. The season started with an NHL lockout, which meant AHL rosters were loaded with NHL talent. "I was thinking, *I'm going to get screwed, so I better fucking be ready*."

Roussel did what he always did. He worked. Nothing fancy. He kept at it during training camp, not that he was remaining all that calm, what with all the NHLers at the AHL camp. "I was thinking, *They are going to cut me. They are actually going to cut me*. So I was pushing, pushing. I was playing better and getting to that sweet spot that I finished at the previous year in Chicago. I was feeling better about myself. I was getting my stride. I was making plays. I was being a pest. I started as a fourth-line centre, and they actually put me in the team apartment. The guys called it 'The PTO Palace.'"

PTO stands for pro tryout. Players who attend camp on a PTO are unsigned free agents, often veterans, taking a low-percentage shot at catching on with a team. So, the PTO Palace was not exactly long-term accommodations. It didn't make Roussel feel all that secure, but it was better than a hotel. "It's for guys that are called up or sent down. They have to put them there, so my thinking was if they don't tell me to get a place, they are going to send me down for sure. I was okay with it because I was in that situation before, but I was thinking, *No days off. I can't take anything for granted.* I started playing better, getting points, starting to generate offence. I always made sure I had an impact on the game, whether I was on the ice or not. I always knew somebody was watching. My thinking was, *Somebody is watching.* I kept that feeling. I kept pushing and pushing."

Roussel was right. The Stars were watching. The team's general manager, Joe Nieuwendyk, and director of player development Les Jackson were watching.

"I think he might've played thirty-eight games in the American League before he got called up, and he just stayed in the NHL," says Turner. It was forty-three in 2012–13, to be exact. Roussel, the kid who had one goal in his first pro season, put up eight goals and eleven assists in those forty-three games with Texas, to go along with 107 PIMs. On February 1, 2013, Roussel scored his first NHL goal in the first of his 607 career NHL games. He had seven minutes and eighteen seconds of ice time that night against the Phoenix Coyotes. Pretty good for a kid who was never drafted, never supposed to be there.

"It's great to know that there are scouts watching guys like me that just have a dream and [eventually get to] play in the NHL. When you look at it, if every player that was drafted made it to the NHL, then there would be no jobs for a guy like me. Our job as players is to think, *I can still play well. I can still get there. I can get hungrier.* It's just about the mindset, the attitude and mindset that you have. That makes the difference.

"A good scout sees beyond the numbers," says Roussel, who retired after the 2021–22 season. "When I got to the pros, I wasn't playing twenty minutes a night. I was playing six or seven minutes a night. Some games, I was playing four minutes a night. I knew from the get-go that I was going to be a fourth-liner if I made the NHL. And I was happy with that. I'm good. I'm good. There are no bad jobs in the NHL. That was the way I saw it."

Shane Turner and the Dallas Stars saw that Roussel was the kind of player they looked for, the kind of player Shane Turner still looks for after a lifetime in the game.

"How do you separate one player from the other?" asked Turner. "That's a really good question. We have some core values that we look for. The way they read the play. Hockey intelligence, we call it, is very high on our list of priorities. How hard a player works, for instance. I will go and I will sit in the rink where I cannot only see the whole rink, but I can see both benches. I can see the interaction of players on the bench and the interaction between players and coaches. That's very important because that translates into whether that kid is going to make himself a better teammate and a better player. So, we do things like that. I go to a lot of practices. I like to go and see who works hard. Who gets along with their teammates in practice. Who is encouraging, who is helping each other out. Are they on early? Do they stay on late? If they stay on late, what are they working on? What are your weaknesses? So, when I see a player that is working hard at his weaknesses, that tells me there's a player that's going to make himself a better player."

As Forbes Kennedy told Turner over fifty years ago, "It's all about how hard you work and being a good teammate."

CHAPTER 11

Old School

Les Binkley

Les Binkley (right) and the author share a moment at Scotiabank Hockey Day in Canada in Owen Sound, Ontario, in January 2023. COURTESY THE AUTHOR

There's a saying that good things come in threes. Or, depending on how you look at the world, maybe you always say bad things come in threes. Whether you look at things in a good or bad way, things did come in threes for hockey lifer Les Binkley.

In his first year of hockey the threes were a knife, a notorious teammate and an explosion.

By the end of his professional hockey life, the threes were Dale Hawerchuk, Teemu Selänne and Jaromír Jágr.

Les Binkley was a small-town kid from Walkerton, Ontario, just trying to make it in the hockey world when he joined the Galt Black Hawks in 1951. Like every other goalie at the time, he was a maskless stand-up puck stopper. In fact, he didn't wear a mask for the first time until years later, after he had already played two years in the National Hockey League. "They cleaned my bridgework out after about six weeks. I got hit right in the mouth with a slapshot off the draw. If you want to lose weight, eat out of a blender," laughs the old goalie.

When he was playing junior in Galt, he counted future Chicago Black Hawks Pete Conacher and Kenny Wharram as his teammates. The big team in Chicago could have taken more of a chance on Binkley, too, but "they were old-school," he says. "They told me I was a good goalie, but that I couldn't see."

Binkley shot back that he had 20/20 vision. The Black Hawks knew Binkley had 20/20 vision . . . with a little help. "They said, 'Why do you wear those funny things in your eyes?'" The "funny things" were contact lenses. Binkley had perfect vision as long as he had his contacts in. But a goalie who needed a little help seeing was not what Chicago was looking for. Years later, Tony Esposito, who also wore contacts, became a Hall of Famer for the Black Hawks. But in Binkley's time, a goalie who needed contacts, or glasses, was a no-go for the Hawks.

With his NHL dreams over, Binkley ended up playing intermediate hockey for his hometown Walkerton Capitals. He was twenty-one years old. Binkley and the Capitals ended up winning the OHA Intermediate B championship. "We played against Sundridge in the finals. We went to almost the end of May."

The magic of a championship, though, was not enough to keep the small-town Capitals alive. The team folded, and Binkley needed a new hockey home. He found one in the fall of 1955 in Baltimore, Maryland, beginning his pro career in the six-team Eastern Hockey League. Besides Baltimore, the rough-and-tumble Eastern League had teams in Washington, DC; Clinton, New York; New Haven, Connecticut; Philadelphia; and, of course Johnstown, Pennsylvania. The rosters were not huge, and most of the players looked exactly the way you would imagine they would look in 1955. They had tight haircuts. They didn't have sideburns. And they all looked like they were ready to get down to business. That's what young Les Binkley was ready to do when he arrived in Maryland to start his professional career. Among his teammates was perhaps the most notorious man to ever play in the Eastern League, John Brophy, the tough-as-nails career minor leaguer and future head coach of the Toronto Maple Leafs.

"He was nuts," says a laughing Binkley of the notorious EHL stick man. "You only went around Brophy once. The second time around, he would hit you right over the head with his stick. Seriously!"

Binkley would look at his teammate, somewhat mortified, but Brophy figured the five-minute penalty he got for smashing his stick over the head of a high-flying opponent was worth it in the long run. "Brophy would say, 'Well, he won't be back again!' You'd say, 'Broph!

You got five minutes!' He'd say, 'Yeah, but the other guy, he's gone for the game.' That's the way Brophy was."

Binkley says Brophy could fight, too. In fact, when a line brawl would break out—and there were more than a few of them in the EHL—Brophy would often help out his goalie. "I fought all the time. Everybody did. Brophy would look over while he was fighting, and if the guy was on top of me, he'd come over and whack the guy and then I'd get on top of the guy. We'd start fighting again. And if I ended up on the bottom again, I would look over at Brophy and he would come over again and do his thing."

It was rough on the ice, and things weren't exactly all that comfortable off the ice, either. When Binkley arrived for training camp, he and five other teammates were put in a room in the basement of a Baltimore hotel. There were six single beds, all lined up side by side, for six hockey players. Among the others in the room with Binkley was Brophy, future Edmonton Oilers head coach John Muckler, Gerry Norman and a couple of others. To pass the time, a few of the guys would play cards. Binkley wasn't a card player, so he'd lie on his bed. It's a good thing he didn't play cards. "One of the guys, he pulls out a knife and he put it down on the card table. And I'm thinking, *I wonder what the hell is going to happen with this.*"

Calmer heads prevailed. The knife stayed on the table. "They were fine," Binkley says, before casually adding, "but then the rink blew up in January.

"It couldn't get more exciting than that."

8-ALARM FIRE DESTROYS ICE RINK, screamed the headline on the front page of the *Baltimore Evening Sun* on January 23, 1956. Under the headline was a picture of complete and total devastation. To the right of the photo, in large type, were the words CLIPPERS LOSE HOME. To call it exciting is an understatement. "And we had to go on the road," said Binkley. "The Hershey Bears gave us uniforms, and instead of playing home games, we played on the road. And they put five of our games in Charlotte."

And that was the start of Binkley's hockey life in Charlotte, North Carolina. The Baltimore Clippers became the Charlotte Clippers. And if any modern player ever has a complaint about the rigours of the road, they should take note of what Les Binkley and his Clippers teammates had to put up with. "The closest team was in Johnstown, Pennsylvania. That was 560 miles away."

Life in the minors has often been described as an endless bus trip. The Charlotte Clippers didn't have a bus. That's right. They were a professional hockey team without a bus. They had four cars. The players did the driving, except for the goalie. And, oh yeah, teams in the EHL only carried one goalie. "I always rode with Muckler and Brophy and another guy. I had to sit in the back seat. I'd say, 'I can't drive.' The players had to take turns. I told them it was too hard on my eyes. So I sat in the back and slept."

One of the biggest challenges for any carload of Clippers was getting to the game on time. "Very seldom would we ever start a game with a complete team. Usually, one car would be delayed because it would be pulled over."

Binkley says the state troopers knew the Clippers' schedule and would be waiting for them. If a carload of speedy Clippers cruised by in the middle of nowhere, the police lights would come on and it would be time to pull over. And there would be a problem as well: To pay the fine, the coppers demanded cash on the spot. The players, who were making $115 a week, wouldn't have enough cash to pay the fine. They would have to call back to Charlotte to get the money wired their way. And they didn't get to wait by the side of the road; they would wait in the local jail. "And these were the old-time jails like you saw on the westerns. It was hilarious. They'd lock up the drivers, and the rest of us would stand around and wait."

There was no sense arguing with cops or the local judge, either. This was small-town USA. When you were pulled over, more often than not you were talking to the cop, the judge and the jury all at once. "The thing was, the state trooper would take off his hat and put on a black robe. He was also the judge. So you couldn't really argue that you weren't speeding."

And that was the start of Les Binkley's professional career. It was a minor-league odyssey with stops in Fort Wayne, Indiana; Toledo, Ohio; Cleveland and San Diego. He made many friends and gathered many stories along the way. "San Diego bought me on a napkin," he says. "We went to practice in Bermuda shorts and sandals, and we'd be on the golf course by twelve noon. It was perfect."

But it didn't last long. By the time Les Binkley's one and only season in San Diego wrapped up, he was thirty-two years old. That's pretty old for a goalie. But after that season, opportunity knocked. The fall of 1967 was on the way, and so were six more teams in the NHL. The Original Six era was over. The expansion era was about to begin. At the age of thirty-three, Binkley became an NHL rookie with the Pittsburgh Penguins. If San Diego in the spring of 1967 was paradise, in the fall of 1967, Pittsburgh was . . . well, Pittsburgh. "Pittsburgh was like Hamilton, with the steel mills everywhere. I had an inch of soot on my car every day. The fans were—well, we didn't have that many, but the ones that showed up were good fans. They were loyal. It was exciting to play in the NHL."

That first year in the NHL had its moments. Like shutting out the Boston Bruins in Boston Garden. "That was pretty exciting, shutting out the Bruins. I had all their numbers. The gallery gods there gave me a standing ovation."

The win came with a bonus, too. Bruins goalies Gerry Cheevers and Eddie Johnston sent Binkley a six-pack after the game. "You were a hero on the bus on your way to the airport. Everybody wants to sit with you because they want to share your beer. Cheesy said, 'I should've given you twelve that night. I didn't know you're going to play so well.'"

Binkley spent five years in Pittsburgh and got to sit by a legend, too—a legend with equally bad eyes. "Tim Horton sat beside me in the dressing room. The thing was, Tim couldn't see very good. He wore contacts, the same as I did. Tim used to say to me, 'If you see the puck coming at my head, yell to me!' I said, 'What makes you think I'm going to see it?'"

Binkley would get to play in the Montreal Forum, too, against his old Cleveland Barons minor-league teammate John Ferguson. "When I played against him in the NHL, he would always come around and whack my rear end because he knew I had no padding there. He was a good friend."

After five seasons with the Penguins, Binkley did what a lot of pros did at the time—he bolted for the WHA. By 1976, he was a forty-one-year-old goalie playing in a hell of a lot of pain. His knees were shot. "The thing was, they made me play, and the players were going over to the coach, begging him to get me out of there. I had to put my hands on top of the net to pull myself up."

In the summer of 1976, a doctor dug into one of Binkley's knees. They removed his kneecap and tied all his tendons together. He could play ball. He could golf. But he could not play hockey anymore. The old goalie was done. But the old goalie had been around the game forever. When you speak with Les Binkley, he talks more about the people he met than the games he played during his pro career.

Soon enough, one of his old teammates called. It was his old friend John Ferguson, who was now the general manager of the New York Rangers. Ferguson asked Binkley to be the Rangers' goalie coach as well as a scout. Binkley didn't wait long to think about his answer. "I said, 'Sure. When do you want me there?' He said, 'Tomorrow.' So, I flew to New York City."

The next phase of Les Binkley's hockey career was now under way. All that knowledge he had accumulated his entire life was now going to be put to the test. He will tell you, though, he had an eye for the game, an eye for players, long before he was even a pro.

"Did you ever see how many people that are goalies are in scouting and even on TV [as commentators]?" said Binkley. "I think if you have a feel for the game, you got it. And I always had that. Even when I was a little kid. I was a rink rat in Owen Sound. I would go to the games back when they had to scrape the ice and they had to flood it by hand. And I'll tell you, there was a guy who was going to be a good goalie. I watched the senior teams come to Owen Sound. You probably never heard of this guy. His brother was an All-Star, a Hall of Famer. He played for the Toronto Marlies. His name was Howie Harvey. He was Doug Harvey's brother. He was stocky, and he really stood up well. But he had some disease that when he sweated, he would break out. He didn't play very long. I saw him; he was really good. This is way back, you know."

Way back, as in the late 1940s. That's when Les Binkley, who would have been a young teenager at the time, saw Harvey play. Yes, Les had an eye for talent. Harvey attended camp with the Maple Leafs. The Society for International Hockey Research says Harvey retired in September 1949 "because of a persistent skin rash." There's another possible reason listed on their website as well, because of "seeing Baz Bastien lose an eye in training camp September 19." Les Binkley could pick 'em from the time he was a kid.

When his adventure with the Rangers began, Binkley would work with the goalies on the big team in New York as well as with those on the team's AHL affiliate in New Haven. Plus, he had to scout. When he was in New Haven, that's when Binkley the goalie coach could instantly transform into Binkley the Rangers scout. He discovered what was, in the late 1970s, pretty much unchartered territory for people looking for the next NHL prospect. "I would go to Yale. Their arena is the shape of a whale," says Binkley. "I went to hockey games at the American colleges for two or three years, and I wouldn't see another scout. Guys didn't scout there until a whole bunch of players started popping up, and then they started going in. But Fergie was way ahead of his time. He had me going to all those colleges.

"There was a lot of talent. And the big thing was, because of their system, they would play Friday and Saturday, but they had phenomenal exercise rooms back then. The football players all used those rooms, too. The players were in great shape. They practised every day for an hour and a half or two hours, and they would only play two games a week. And the college player started with no [centre-ice] red line. It was pretty exciting hockey. It was wide open, and these guys really worked on their skills."

Les didn't stick with the Rangers for too long, though. On June 1, 1978, his buddy John Ferguson was fired. The Rangers brought in Fred "The Fog" Shero, who had won two Cups with the Broad Street Bullies, as the new general manager and head coach. That meant Shero was in charge when the Rangers made their selections two weeks later, on June 15, at the 1978 NHL Amateur Draft. As was the custom at the time, the draft was held at the Queen Elizabeth Hotel in Montreal. Shero wasn't exactly overly involved in the selections.

"After about the sixth or seventh round, we were sitting there. Up pops Fred Shero and Mikey Nykoluk [Shero's assistant coach], and they say, 'You guys handle the rest of the draft the way you think. We have a flight shortly.' And they left. Can you believe that?!"

That would not happen today. In 1978, you could also draft for as long as you wanted to. You could pick until there was nobody left that you wanted. That year's draft didn't end until the Montreal Canadiens made the one and only pick of the twenty-second round: Doug Robb, 234th overall. Once Shero left, Binkley and the rest of the Rangers scouts did whatever they wanted. They didn't end their day until the fifteenth round.

The Rangers made sixteen picks that day. Their first selection wasn't until the twenty-sixth spot. But they still got a good player in Don Maloney, who would go on to score 564 points in 765 NHL games. And you could see the Binkley effect, too. The Rangers selected eight NCAA players in the draft, practically unheard of at that time. Remarkably, the eight players the Rangers took from US colleges were the second most by any team in 1978. Montreal took the most at ten. Four of the Rangers selections went on to play in the NHL. The best of the bunch came with the ninety-third pick. Tom Laidlaw was a defenceman at Northern Michigan. He ended up playing in 705 regular-season NHL games, most of them in his almost seven full seasons on the Rangers blue line.

It's not like Fred Shero was impressed with the draft that day, though. Before leaving, he told reporters, "Don't ask me. I don't know anything about them. Ask my scouts."

The media wouldn't have long to ask Les Binkley about the draft. With his buddy Ferguson gone, he soon got the news that he was out as well. "We all got fired by New York after the draft."

Binkley wasn't out of work for long. Ferguson was hired by the WHA's Winnipeg Jets on November 22, 1978. Soon enough, he hired Binkley as the Jets' goalie coach and scout. Binkley was now back in the WHA. But not for long—the Jets joined the NHL as part of the merger on June 22, 1979. Binkley stayed in Winnipeg for eleven seasons. He would scout Ontario and, as always, would head down to the USA to check out all those under-the-radar college kids he liked. "On a Thursday, I would whip into Windsor and see the Spitfires play, but then I'd go to the college games, too. It was the CCHA [Central Collegiate Hockey Association] back then—Michigan, Michigan State. And these college coaches became good friends of mine. Red Berenson was at Michigan and Ron Mason was at Michigan State. He would come up to Goderich in the summer and fish."

Binkley and the Jets struck it big at the 1981 NHL draft. Their first couple of NHL seasons were difficult, and that is being polite. When WHA teams joined the NHL, they were stripped of their established talent. If a player's rights were previously owned by an NHL team, they could reclaim that player from the incoming WHA team. The Jets finished the 1980–81 season with a 9–57–14 record. That's right, the Jets had nine wins. In those days, there was no draft lottery, which meant Winnipeg would pick first overall in 1981. They did not make a mistake.

A kid from Toronto had lit up the Quebec Major Junior League the previous season. The Cornwall Royals, representing the easternmost city in the Ontario, had a bit of a strange set-up. They took part in the Ontario Hockey League's draft but played in the Q. The result was a team made up mostly of Ontario kids, playing against players and teams from Quebec, and Dale Hawerchuk was the best of the bunch. "I saw a lot of Dale. I went to Cornwall quite a bit," says Binkley.

"Dale wasn't attracting a lot of eyeballs at the beginning . . . and we couldn't figure it out. Dale was a good hockey player. He jumped off the page. You know yourself, with the top players, you have no problem picking them up. It's the ones that go later on in the draft. Fergie used to say if you need a program to watch your own area, which for me was Ontario, then you haven't seen the players enough."

Hawerchuk was the consensus number one pick in 1981. The Jets had offers for the pick, but they stuck to their guns. So, as Bentley says, taking a player like Hawerchuk was the easy part. With their second pick of the draft, twenty-second overall, they took Hawerchuk's Cornwall teammate Scott Arniel. "Scotty was a good two-way player, not exceptional like Hawerchuk. Hawerchuk was such a super guy."

The following year, the Jets got a gem in the third round—a Junior A kid who was heading south to play NCAA hockey at Bowling Green. Dave Ellett became a mainstay on Winnipeg's blue line and played in over 1,100 NHL games. Once again, Binkley nabbed a college kid. He goes right back into scout mode when he talks about Ellett, a man his buddies call Roy—as in Roy Hobbs from the movie *The Natural*. Yes, Ellett could do anything, including play a solid game from the point. "I played with his father, Bobby, in Cleveland. I knew the family pretty well. He was a good, solid player. There was nothing flashy, but he got the job done. He had a good shot from the point—a nice, low shot. He wasn't going to kill the guy standing in front. It's pretty hard to tip it in when it's six feet high."

Like any good scout, Binkley would poke around, ask questions. He had his special go-to guys inside the rinks. "It's funny, you know, when you go to these private schools in the US and you talk to the guys who work around the rink, some of them give you pretty good insight on the players. The Zamboni drivers have some great insight on players. You'd say, 'How's what's his name? What kind of a kid is he?' Well, they'd tell me he comes late, or they tell me he's the kind of kid that you have to turn the lights off to get him off the ice. He just loves to play."

By the time the 1988 draft came around, Binkley was a veteran member of the Jets staff. That did not mean that he always got his way, though. The Jets selected tenth overall that year. Winnipeg had had some luck with Europeans in the previous few years, nabbing Teppo Numminen and Fredrik Olausson with second- and fourth-round picks. But the Jets had never used a first-rounder on a European—until, that is, 1988. The pick, to Binkley at least, was a mystery. "Well, the big thing is, naturally you see your own area more than you see the West or the East. Our job is to outline the players in our area."

That, of course, meant that if a scout really liked a player in his area, he would have to go to bat for the kid. Usually, even if you were scouting Ontario, you could get a look at kids from the East and West as well. In 1988, though, Europe was pretty much no man's land if you were an Ontario scout like Binkley. "We used to have a guy who went to Europe, but we never saw the European players. We used to have awful discussions on who to take at the pre-meetings. We would almost come to blows. You were fighting for your guy in your area."

Binkley didn't win the fight in 1988. The Jets selected Teemu Selänne out of Finland. Four years after he was drafted, the future Hall of Famer scored seventy-six goals as a rookie with the Jets.

By that time, Bentley was scouting for the Pittsburgh Penguins. He joined Pittsburgh for the 1989–90 season, and stayed scouting with them for ten seasons. Binkley's first draft with the Pens was in 1990. Owen Nolan went first overall, followed by Petr Nedvěd, Keith Primeau and Mike Ricci. The Penguins had the fifth pick. They had their list, and they were going with a European. Binkley was more than cool with the selection. He had seen this super-sized kid play in a few tournaments on this side of the Atlantic. "It wasn't much of a discussion when it came to Jaromír. Did you see where we drafted Jágr? Fifth! How could the other four teams pass up on him? We didn't go to Europe, but he came over here and played in some tournaments, and he was phenomenal. I didn't see all the games he had in North America, but I saw some of them. Yeah, he stood out."

Les got his first Stanley Cup ring with the Pittsburgh Penguins in 1991. He got his second when they won again in 1992. Those two rings, which he still wears, are a great reminder of his time with the Pens. He lost a few other mementoes. "Jágr had signed some cards and everything for me back when I was scouting for Pittsburgh, but I don't know where the hell they are."

Binkley retired from scouting after the 1998–99 season. He had attended twenty-three straight NHL drafts, practising his craft. That's a long way from a knife, a notorious stick man and an arena explosion in the Eastern League. "Do you know what the sad part is? I made more money scouting than I did playing. Now, does that make sense? I enjoyed myself."

CHAPTER 12

Hollywood Knocks

Rick Knickle

Rick Knickle during his Junior days with the Brandon Wheat Kings.

Rick Knickle phoned his then mother-in-law when he signed a NHL contract with the Los Angeles Kings in February 1993. His mother-in-law was working in the media back home in Brandon, Manitoba. She put the news out on the wire, and then Knickle's hotel phone started ringing. "I sat down for lunch at twelve o'clock. My phone never stopped ringing for eight hours. Everybody from everywhere were phoning to try and get an interview with me," says the former scout for the Nashville Predators, Arizona Coyotes and Columbus Blue Jackets.

It wasn't a big-money deal. It was for $68,000 for the rest of the season. The Kings threw in some bonuses. Knickle would get something like $500 for a win and $2,000 for every shutout he got. That was pretty decent money for a guy who had spent his entire career up until that point in the minors.

The "up until that point" is why sports reporters from around North America wanted to talk. He was thirty-two years old. He had played for fourteen professional teams over his twelve-and-a-half-year minor-league career. He had never played in the NHL. Now that was about to change for Knickle, who had thought his NHL dreams were over.

"By the time I was twenty-seven or twenty-eight, my thoughts on the NHL were gone. I thought, *There is no way I'm going to make it. I'm just too old. I haven't done enough.*"

But Knickle, who started his professional career in 1979–80 with the IHL's Muskegon Mohawks, just kept playing. It was not like he had a lot of options. "I had nothing else. I got my Grade 12. I don't have any skills to do anything. Hockey was my life. I made it my life; if I didn't play, then I'd probably get into coaching and get into something along the lines of hockey, because that was all I knew. By the time I was twenty-seven years old, I started to relax. I just started playing for myself, not playing for my affiliate team that didn't give a shit about me."

Following a stellar junior career with the Brandon Wheat Kings, the Buffalo Sabres took Knickle 116th overall in the 1979 NHL draft. He was driving around Brandon when he heard the news on the radio. Later that day, he got a phone call from a hockey legend who was coaching the Sabres at the time, Roger Neilson. "I had a good year . . . and I didn't know Roger was an ex-goalie. He phoned my dad. He said, 'Rick is out in Brandon.' 'Okay, I'll get a hold of him out there.' Roger phones me—and I should explain first, we had a lot of pranksters on our team. I pick up the phone and the guy says, 'It's Roger Neilson.' I'm pissed off. I mean, I don't know it's Roger Neilson. I think it's a buddy of mine on my team acting like he's Neilson."

Knickle didn't give Roger Neilson anything. It was short, "whatever"-type answers to anything he had to say. "Basically, all I said was 'Yeah. Okay. Yeah.' He told me, 'We'll send you some stuff.' I said, 'Great.'"

Knickle hung up. Then his phone rang again. This time, it was his dad on the line from the Maritimes. He wanted to know if Neilson had called. "Oh, fuck. I'm glad I didn't say anything derogatory to him. And then I realized the voice on the phone did sound kind of like Neilson."

Fourteen years later, Rick was sitting in front of a guy he met at his first Buffalo Sabres camp. It was Rick Dudley.

When Knickle started his pro career, he didn't really think he was ever going to play in the NHL. "I wasn't thinking I was going to get to the NHL. I just thought because of my small-town mentality that it was just so far out of my realm," says Knickle, who grew up in Greenwood, Nova Scotia, playing on teams with his much older brothers.

And for twelve years after he left the Wheat Kings, Knickle was right—he was not going to the NHL. But Dudley, who was now the head coach of the San Diego Gulls of the International League, had something he wanted to say. He was sitting behind his desk, reading the newspaper. He took a peek over the paper, looked at Knickle and said, “If an NHL team came and wanted you to go to the NHL, would you go?”

Thirty-two-year-old Rick Knickle was having none of it. Sure, he was one of the top goalies in the IHL, a high-flying development league, in 1992–93, but he was in no mood to get chirped by Dudley. “I said, ‘That’s pretty funny, Duds. What do you want?’”

Dudley was quite serious: If an NHL team came looking for Knickle to sign up, would he go? That’s when Knickle suddenly got serious. “‘Duds, I’ve been looking for an opportunity for twelve fucking years! I’m playing the best I’ve played in my whole career right now.’ We had a good team, but I was just on fire. He told me, ‘Sit tight. It’s going to happen.’”

His numbers were excellent for the Gulls. He had a 2.17 goals-against average and a .909 save percentage in forty-one games. The old pro was settled in and playing great hockey. Dudley didn’t tell him what team was interested, but it didn’t take him long to find out. He left the coach’s room and ran into his teammate Keith Gretzky. That would be Wayne’s younger brother. Knickle told Gretzky to keep it on the down low, but an NHL team was interested in signing him. Keith already knew. And he knew the team. The Gretzky brothers had been talking. News of Knickle’s stellar play had made its way to number 99.

Knickle held tight and went out and got an agent. He didn’t even have one at the time. He got Tom Laidlaw, a former player who was interning for super-agent Michael Barnett, to represent him. Knickle kept stopping pucks. A week went by. Nothing happened. Then Knickle went to play in the IHL All-Star Game on February 3, 1993, in Phoenix. He was told the Kings had eyes in the stands: "I knew they were there, I knew this is my only opportunity, so I stopped twenty-four of twenty-five."

Knickle played an almost perfect period and a half for the Western All-Stars. "All the reporters told me afterwards that I should've gotten the MVP, but they didn't want to give it to me because I was old."

Instead, eighteen-year-old Sergei Krivokrasov, who scored two goals for the East in their 7–5 win, was handed the award. He received $1,000 and a set of golf clubs. Knickle, a lifelong minor leaguer, could have used both the cash and the clubs. "As we were shaking hands after the game, he's already got the golf clubs over his shoulder. I thought, *Those are mine. You don't even golf!*"

Knickle just kept playing for the Gulls. There was still no call from the Kings. One night on a road trip in Cincinnati, Knickle met up with Cincy goalie Troy Gamble and his teammate Craig Coxe. When Knickle got back to his hotel room that night, his phone was flashing. He had a message. It was from Rick Dudley. He wanted to know where the hell Knickle was. He wanted the goalie to call him in the morning. Knickle had an inkling of what the coach was calling about, and he couldn't wait. It was one in the morning, but he called his coach right away. "The Kings want to do a deal," said Dudley. "'Get the fuck out of here! Really? They want to sign me?'"

They did. Knickle got the deal done. GOALIE KNICKLE FINALLY WILL GET HIS SHOT, read the headline in the *Los Angeles Times* on February 17, 1993. OPPORTUNITY KNOCKS IN THE KNICK OF TIME was the headline in the Vancouver *Province*. By the time the headlines made the paper the next day, Knickle was already in Minnesota.

He backed up Kelly Hrudey in a 10–5 Kings win. "I go in there and I put the jersey on just to go on the ice for the practice and face NHL shots again. Not training camp. These are NHL guys, and I could see the difference. When I put the jersey on and skated around for warmup, it was just surreal. Putting that jersey on, especially that one—the LA Kings! I was playing with Wayne. The aura of that team and that dressing room was really special. And everyone on that team knew a lot about me before, just because guys had played in the minors or whatever. But to play on that team and understand that I was wanted, and they respected me, and they brought me there because they felt that I could help their team . . . that meant a lot."

The next day, in Chicago, Knickle played in his first NHL game, starting against the Blackhawks. "The first save I made was forty seconds into the game. I caught the puck. It was one of those [situations where you think] *Oh fuck. I can't drop it. What am I going to do?*"

Knickle held on. The ref blew his whistle, then made his way to Knickle. It was Paul Stewart, the former player turned ref. Knickle, in fact, knew him from the days when both of them were in the Buffalo Sabres organization. "'Okay, Knick, you can do whatever you want tonight, babe. This is your night.' And I told him, 'Oh, fuck. Thanks, Stewey. I needed that.'"

Knickle took a breath and took a moment to let it all sink in. He was in the NHL. But he was still playing the game he knew. He looked around, and he didn't have to look too far to find some well-wishing fans. "A few signs said, 'Welcome.' 'Congratulations.' There were a lot of people that knew me and probably saw me play against the [IHL Chicago] Wolves. That was really surreal, to play in that stadium for my first NHL game."

The rest of the night didn't go as planned. Knickle kept the Kings in the game through the first two periods; LA was down 3–1 after forty minutes. The third period was all Chicago. Knickle had been battling a bout of food poisoning, and it caught up to him: "I had no gas in the tank in the third. I was cramping up big time. It was 3–1 for them, and I was cramping up. I thought, *I'm not coming out, no way!* They scored four, and three of them were just so bad. I couldn't even see the puck."

Even though he lost, Knickle was feeling good. He knew he could play in the NHL. He got his next shot four nights later in Tampa. And there was good news. His mom and dad were there. His dad, whom Knickle calls the Walter Gretzky of Nova Scotia, had been waiting for this moment for a long time. "My dad got an ulcer because of me," says Knickle. How? Because every summer at the Brightwood Golf Club, all the other golfers would ask George Knickle, "How's Rick doing? Is Rick going to make it this year?"

George would not have to answer that question anymore. With his parents in the stands, Knickle got his first NHL win and was named the first star of the game when the Kings beat the Lightning on March 22, 1993. Rick made forty-three saves in a 5–2 win. Wayne Gretzky, the game's second star, had four points. George Knickle had first told his son about this kid named Wayne from Brantford after seeing him play at the Quebec International Pee Wee tournament in 1972. Now the two were teammates. George's son was an NHLer. Just like Walter Gretzky, George Knickle had flooded a backyard rink for his boys. "I knew my dad was right there on my shoulder throughout my career. It was unbelievable when I finally got a chance to tell him I was going to the NHL," says Rick, who still gets emotional talking about his dad watching him play. Making the NHL was almost like a thank you from the son to his father, no matter how long the journey took.

"To hug my dad after that game," Rick tells me over the phone, was special. "I've never really hugged my dad in my life . . . I still get choked up about it."

The wins kept coming for Knickle. He was a rookie, an old one, finally living the NHL dream.

"I loved playing cards on the bus in the minor leagues. It's on the bus. But in the NHL, it was on the plane. I get on the plane and there are seven guys playing cards. I didn't jump right in. I was the guy who said, 'Hey, anybody need some change?' I knew my place. I was a rookie and I'm the oldest guy on that team. All of a sudden, one guy is out of the game and doesn't want to play anymore. And I thought, *I got money now.* We didn't play for big money—twenty dollars and a thousand-dollar pot max, probably, but for me it was a big deal. Can I get into these million-dollar guys' pockets?' Absolutely."

Rick Knickle went 6–4 with a 3.95 goals-against average and an .880 save percentage in ten games with LA. He stuck with the team throughout the playoffs, all the way to the Stanley Cup Final. The Montreal Canadiens won that series, 4–1, winning the Cup that year. Knickle played in four games for the Kings the following season and then never played in the NHL again. He went back to the IHL, suiting up for Phoenix, Las Vegas, Detroit and Milwaukee.

Late in his career, he got a call from a Bruins scout named Scott Bradley. Boston had the first and eighth picks in the 1997 draft. Bradley told Knickle they planned on taking Joe Thornton with the number one pick, but they weren't sure what they were going to do at number eight. Bradley wanted to know a little bit about a teenager playing for the Detroit Vipers named Sergei Samsonov. Knickle, who was playing for Milwaukee at the time, was more than familiar with the speedy kid who was playing pro at just seventeen. "I said,

'Perfect.' I had played against Samsonov twice, and I played in the NHL by that time two years before, and Samsonov scared the shit out of me. When he got the puck on the rush, he had [Connor] McDavid speed."

Knickle told Bradley what he thought of Samsonov, capping it off with "Samsonov could play in the NHL for you next year. That's how good I think he is."

Bradley relayed the message to the Bruins. He told them that Rick Knickle had told him that this Samsonov kid was the real deal. "I talked to a goalie who played against Samsonov, which is what we would do in scouting."

And just like that, Rick's scouting career was almost born. He tried to get a job with the Bruins that summer, but it didn't pan out. Still, he knew he wanted to scout. His dad scouted. Knickle says he got his scouting ability from his dad. When his dad saw Wayne Gretzky at the 1972 pee wee tournament in Quebec, he even made a note beside Gretzky's name in the program. He wrote: "1979 draft may be too small." (By the way, Knickle showed the program to Gretzky when they were teammates in LA.)

Knickle's scouting career was born when the Nashville Predators hired him to scout the West. Knickle was based out of Manitoba, where he had played junior. For years, in fact, he would return to Brandon in the summers to work at hockey schools. He'd keep an eye on Kelly McCrimmon's Wheat Kings, too, so he was more than familiar with the junior landscape. And as a long-time pro who had won an IHL championship, a WHL title and had been to the Memorial Cup and Stanley Cup Finals, he figured he knew what he was looking for.

"I used to help Kelly McCrimmon in his training camp for years in Brandon. I'd be in their scouting meetings. I'd give my scouting evaluations about players, and I worked with the goalies. I worked with Trevor Kidd and those guys, helping them out of camp, evaluating them and working them on the ice."

Knickle got to work. Between 2000 and 2003, the Preds hit it out of the park as far as getting guys out of the WHL. In 2000, they selected Scottie Hartnell sixth overall. In 2001, they nabbed Dan Hamhuis at twelve and Jordin Tootoo ninety-eighth. In 2002, it was Scottie Upshall at six. In 2003, the Preds stole Shea Weber forty-ninth overall. "After the first couple of good drafts, [Nashville GM] David Poile kept looking down the table at me. You start to think like a GM, trying to build a team. I won five championships in my life; I had an idea of what makes your team win, the skill you need, the competitiveness. And it doesn't hurt to have good goaltending."

By 2003, Knickle was the Preds' assistant director of amateur scouting. He had an eye on the West. He was part of the Nashville brain trust, submitting reports, sitting at the draft table, sitting in on player interviews. In 1979, when Knickle was drafted, there was no such thing as player interviews. By the time he was scouting, they were ingrained as part of the process. "We ask kids questions all the time at drafts. We ask them anything. 'Who do you think you are?' 'What type of player do you think you are?' 'Who would you like to play like?' And some kids would just throw shit out there. You can always spot the fakers. I always say, 'Oh, really? You're not looking in the mirror. You have no idea what type of player you are.'

"We had one guy come in the room once. He's got his suit on and he's fucking sweating. He comes in and grabs the water and drinks. It was a big water jug. He sits down and he's huffing and puffing."

Knickle and the Preds wanted to know what was going on with this kid. He was eighteen years old. He was in stellar shape. But he was drained. He was covered in sweat from head to toe. "We looked at our list to see who interviewed him before us. It was San Jose. They pretty much take you and beat you up. He got beaten up. He told us, 'I hope you guys are going to be easy on me.' We were an expansion team. We were friendly, everybody's good. Kumbaya. We didn't ask any hard questions."

Rick and a few of the other Preds scouts had to figure out what they were doing. If they wanted good answers from these prospects, they had to figure out how to ask good questions. "I was asking the questions and giving the answers at the same time to the kids. I'd ask, 'Hey, what do you think you got to work on?' Then I'd add, 'Your skating?' We weren't skilled at asking questions and interviewing. We weren't detectives. What did David Poile do? He went and got an older guy who taught us how to ask questions, open-enders. 'Give me a time in your career when you thought of yourself being a leader—give me an example.' This guy really helped us learn to ask questions."

And some questions, no matter how simple they might have seemed, produced some answers that left the scouts in stitches, like the time one prospect was asked, "Of anybody dead or alive, who would you like to go for dinner with?"

The kid sat there and thought. Usually, in a hockey player, a question like this could produce an answer like Wayne Gretzky or Rocket Richard. Maybe a kid would say Jesus Christ or Muhammad Ali. This kid thought for a second . . . and then he said the name of the day's top female country star. "Why her?" he was asked.

"Because she's hot."

Not "I love her music," or "I love Nashville" or "I loved her last album." Just "because she's smoking hot."

These interviews, remember, are taking place with eighteen-year-old boys.

Some teams, Knickle says, do try to get pretty deep. "Some teams really try to create the atom bomb. What do you think, you're asking questions that everybody else doesn't ask? You think you're smarter than everybody else?"

The interview is just part of the overall process, part of trying to find out if a kid is a good fit for your organization. "I don't believe in taking somebody right off the chart based on an interview, unless we hear other shit that follows up that means that this guy could be a dick for a teammate. I don't know too many guys who come out of an interview and we all think, *Man, I hate that guy. Take him off the list.* The odd one, but very, very few. I mean, these kids are so groomed. They're so groomed by the agents and by everybody else."

One kid who still sticks with Rick Knickle is a player the Nashville Predators took a chance on in the fourth round in 2001. It was Jordin Tootoo, who grew up in Rankin Inlet, Nunavut. He didn't play organized hockey until he was eleven. "When I interviewed Jordin, I said, 'Jordin, you started out so much later than everybody. How do you do in school?' He said, 'I'm about a ninety average.' So, I said, 'You're fairly smart.' 'Yeah, I'm street-smart, too. I'm going to catch up with all these other guys that are developed ahead of me.' And I believed him."

Knickle believed him because he had known Tootoo since he was fourteen years old. As Knickle mentioned, he used to help out McCrimmon and the Brandon Wheat Kings when he was home in the summers. One year, there were some bantam prospects working out for the Wheat Kings. Knickle arrived at the rink. He was going to coach one of the teams made up of fourteen- and fifteen-year-olds. He looked out on the ice, and that is when he saw Tootoo for the first time. "Jordin was on my team. I'm watching him skate around and warm up. He is snapping pucks! He's fourteen."

Knickle didn't know who the kid was yet. He asked McCrimmon. "Oh, that's Jordin Tootoo," McCrimmon told Knickle. "He's only been playing organized hockey for three years." "I said, 'Where is he from?' He says, 'The north pole.' 'Get out of here.' I'm watching him skate around warmup, snapping pucks. He doesn't have to conk it and shoot it. He just snapped it. And I thought, *Holy fuck!*"

Knickle was impressed. Tootoo came off the ice after the warmup. The game was about to start. But first, Tootoo had a question for Knickle: "Are we allowed to fight?" Knickle was an old WHL guy. He knew the answer was yes. Tootoo was game. "Okay, I'm going to do it."

It didn't take Jordin long to find a partner. He went out and collided with his future Wheat Kings teammate Reagan Leslie. Both of them were looking to make an impression. "They dropped the gloves. They were just going at it. They were chucking them."

When the fight ended, Tootoo skated back to his bench. He had a little cut over his eye. Knickle took a look. "Jordin, you've done that before, correct?" Tootoo took a quick look back at Knickle and proudly stated, "Yeah, and I'm going to do it again."

"I pencilled him in my little notepad. I have two fucking years to wait for this guy [before he was eligible to be drafted]! And he goes out there again and fights Reagan Leslie again, and then he beats him up. I started to follow his career."

Tootoo started his junior career in the Manitoba Junior League as a fifteen-year-old. He had thirty-seven points in forty-seven games. The real story was how he played. He put up 251 penalty minutes and ran over everybody. Eventually, he made his way to Brandon and joined the Wheat Kings. He was a five-foot-nine, 195-pound dynamo. By his draft year, he was a wrecking ball. "I thought, *I'm going to get to see him in his draft year.* He hits a guy behind the net and the guy gets the old weebly wobbles. He can't fall down. And I see this guy after the game, and he's got his fucking arm in a sling and his eye is all cut up. Jordin hit him so fucking hard that he almost put him in the first row."

But Knickle wanted to know if the kid could do more than hit. "I'm watching him play and everything's going well. He can score, he has offence. And Kelly's telling me all about him. He starts to move up the ladder in the lineup. We go to our [scouting] meetings halfway through the year, and pretty much everybody else in our organization thought that he was just an energy guy."

Knickle was loving everything that Tootoo was doing. Some of the other Nashville scouts were not convinced: "Another scout who was at the end of the table didn't say much. He was one of those guys who brings the teacher an apple. He dresses nice and all that stuff." The scout spoke up and said Tootoo was no better than an OHL player that had a reputation for just running around and hitting everything. He said Tootoo just ran around on the ice but had no skill. "I had to battle against this other scout," says Knickle. "Tootoo started to play the point on the power play. Kelly put him on the point on the power play. He could see the ice."

The 2001 NHL draft took place on June 23 and 24 in Sunrise, Florida. The first three rounds took place on the twenty-third. The rest of the draft took place on Sunday the twenty-fourth. The Preds' first selection of the draft was a winner—Dan Hamhuis at twelfth overall. Nashville then picked thirty-third and forty-second. By the time their fourth pick of the day came up, at number seventy-five overall, Tootoo was still available. Nashville also held the seventy-sixth pick. "This is how you have to manufacture your pick's value," Knickle tells me. "We had picks number seventy-five and seventy-six. So if everybody in the organization thinks that that seventy-sixth pick is a flyer, we can take a flyer on a Jordin Tootoo–type player. I didn't think so. I wanted him as a legit player there at seventy-six. I battled for him for months. We were at the table with the seventy-fifth pick."

The Predators selected Denis Platonov at number seventy-five. With the exception of three games with the AHL's Milwaukee Admirals, the centre played his entire pro career in Russia. But the Preds held the seventy-sixth pick, too. Maybe Knickle could get Tootoo there. "We call a time-out because there was a guy on our list that we had ranked about fifteen picks ahead of Jordin that hadn't been taken yet. We had him rated in the second round."

Knickle had never seen this kid play. Another Preds scouts, Greg Royce, was a big fan and had seen him play in person. "Greg had seen him, and he loved him. It was a battle between me and Greg."

Knickle wanted Tootoo. Greg wanted the other guy. "After a while, you can tell scouts are really getting frustrated. They will throw shit out there that doesn't mean anything. Greg says to me—and I know him really well, I like him—'My guy is better than your guy!' And I said, 'You can't say that, Royce, because you've never even seen Tootoo. I haven't seen your guy. You haven't seen my guy. Don't tell me your guy is better than my guy. You don't know!'"

Argue all you want—the list is the list and the Preds had spent months working on it. "Once you do your list, it's done, and you can't sit there and think, *Oh, fuck! We got to take this guy!* He's below that guy. You already went over this for months and months and months. We took Greg's guy at seventy-six, and I agreed with the list. But I had never seen the guy. If we put the guy on our list at the wrong spot, then that's up to the guy who liked him." The player the Preds took with that seventy-sixth pick was an Austrian, Oliver

Setzinger. With the exception of twenty-one games for the AHL's Milwaukee Admirals in 2007–08, he played his entire professional career in Europe.

That was it for day one. Rounds four through nine would take place the next day. The Preds brass headed back to their hotel. "And I am fucking pissed," says Knickle. "And I don't get pissed often, but I am fucking pissed because we were going to take Jordin Tootoo at seventy-six, but because Oliver Setzinger was still there, we took him.

"But something must have been bothering Poile, because he made a point of coming to see me. 'What do I have to do to get Jordin Tootoo for you?'"

The Preds were going to have to wait until the twelfth pick of the fourth round to get Tootoo. Could they wait that long? Would Tootoo still be there?

"Anaheim had two picks early in the fourth. An Anaheim part-time scout in the West was Brandon's head scout. He drafted Tootoo to the Wheat Kings. So, he was the only guy besides me who knew Jordin inside and out. I knew he would take him. I told David, 'You're going to have to trade with Philadelphia.'"

Philadelphia had the opening pick of the fourth round. Poile left and tracked down Flyers general manager Bobby Clarke. "David comes back in, and he said, 'We will flip-flop picks and we will give Philly our third next year.' I said, 'David, I love third-round picks. Those are my meat and potatoes.' Those are the guys I identify and pick. A lot of guys in those areas turn out to be good third-, fourth-line and possibly second-line guys. I said, 'Go get a better deal if you can get a better deal.'"

Poile left to talk to Clarke again. When he came back, he had a new offer. The Preds would send their fourth-, fifth- and seventh-round picks on Sunday to Philly in exchange for their fourth-round pick—ninety-eighth overall. Yes, the first pick of the fourth round. Poile had his deal and Knickle had his man—Tootoo. "I looked at my list and I got no fucking guys I like in that range. We ended up doing the deal. And you should've heard that room. 'You always get your way, Knick.'

"I said, 'Listen! Jordin is going to be a hard guy to send down. We need to get a culture, and I don't want guys to run around.' I tried to compare him to somebody. I thought, *Is he a Mike Keane or is he a Rob DiMaio?*"

He was neither. He was Tootoo. He made the Preds right out of junior in the fall of 2003 and eventually became known as the Tootoo Train. He played on the third and fourth lines.

"Whenever we'd have an injury, he would move up to the first line with Paul Kariya. Tootoo was fucking good. He wouldn't hit anybody when he was on the first line. He would play the game. As a fourth-line guy, he thought, *I'm just going to run and cause havoc and if I get the chance, I can bury it.* But as a top-line guy he knew—*I'm not going to run around.*"

Tootoo became a star during his eight years in Nashville. He played in 486 regular-season games for the Preds and another thirty-nine in the playoffs. He followed his Nashville tenure with stops in New Jersey, Detroit and Chicago. He had sixty-five goals and ninety-six assists for 161 points in 723 career NHL games, to go along with 1,010 penalty minutes. He is also a bestselling author who wrote the story of becoming the NHL's first Inuk player. He shared the stories of the suicide of his brother Terence and of his road to sobriety.

Tootoo hit almost everything in sight when he played. He was the kind of guy the crowd loved, the kind of guy a once-upon-a-time thirty-three-year-old NHL rookie goalie just loved to find during his scouting career. "That's the job of the scouts—to get the glue guys. My mom can come to a game, and I'll say, 'Mom, who's the best player out here?' And she knows. But I can say, 'Oh, there's a guy that's a fourth-rounder! Oh yeah!' I did it all my life."

CHAPTER 13

From the Minors to the Majors

Archie Henderson

Archie Henderson (far right) on the night he was honoured by the Western Canada Professional Hockey Scouts Foundation in the summer of 2024. Henderson is joined by fellow scout Bruce Haralson (left) and Hockey Hall of Famer Ken Holland (middle). COURTESY ARCHIE HENDERSON

"A pro scout is an opinionator," begins Archie Henderson. "And he is an information gatherer. And he gets his opinions from the information he gathers and what he sees."

Henderson would know. He was a pro scout in the NHL for over three decades. He eventually worked his way up to be the Edmonton Oilers' director of pro scouting and retired in the summer of 2022. That gig with the Oilers was the final job in a hockey journey that began for him as a young kid in Calgary. His pro career, though, almost took an extreme detour, at least in his mind. Once upon a time, a young Archie Henderson thought he was on his way to the military.

Henderson played his junior hockey for the Lethbridge Broncos and the Victoria Cougars of what was known in the mid-1970s as the Western Canada Hockey League. These days, it is better known as the Western Hockey League, aka the WHL. When the six-foot, six-inch Henderson wrapped up his fourth major junior season in the spring of 1977, he was eligible for the NHL draft. If a team was looking for a big winger who could rack up a few points and a whole lot more penalty minutes—Henderson had 208 in just forty-seven games for Victoria in 1976–77—Henderson was their man.

When the season ended, Henderson did what he always did, and what no modern draft-eligible player would do: He took a summer job at a bakery on the overnight shift. "I worked the night shift simply because I got twenty-five cents an hour more working the night shift. My uncle was the foreman. He would always hire me every summer."

When the NHL draft came around, it was not a major concern for Henderson. He did what he usually did and went to the factory for his graveyard shift. When he arrived home at around eight in the morning, his mother was anxiously waiting for him at the back door of the family home. "You got to get in here right away," she told Archie.

"I said, 'What's the matter?' And my mother said, 'We just got a phone call from a General McNab in Washington, DC. You've been drafted!' And I'm looking at her and I'm going, 'I can't get drafted. I'm Canadian.'"

Archie's mother didn't think there was much they could do about it. "Well, it's General McNab in Washington. And here's his number and you're supposed to call him," she told her twenty-year-old hockey player and part-time bakery employee.

Henderson was adamant. He once again looked at his mom and repeated the words, "They can't draft me. I'm Canadian."

Archie didn't dare dial the number. It didn't matter—the phone in the Henderson home kept ringing. "I didn't phone him for three days, but he kept calling. He kept calling the house and I wouldn't answer the phone."

After a few days of the phone constantly ringing, Henderson felt he could not hide anymore. He picked up the phone to talk to the general. "I pick up the phone and he's on the other end. He goes, 'Oh no no. It's the general manager, Max McNab, from the Washington Capitals.' And I go, 'Oh, great.'"

McNab told Archie that the Capitals had chosen him with their tenth-round pick in the 1977 NHL draft. Henderson was quite relieved he would not be heading overseas; perhaps just across the continent to DC. If he was naive enough to think he'd been drafted into the army, he was pretty green when it came to understanding what being drafted by the Capitals meant as well. Henderson waited a second or two, and then simply asked Max McNab, "Are you going to send me a contract?"

The answer, of course, was no. But the good news was Archie Henderson would get a chance to earn a contract. That draft, though—the hockey one—was the furthest thing from his mind that summer. Prospects these days obsess over the draft for years, Henderson at the time had other things on his mind. "The only thing that was on my mind was making the extra twenty-five cents an hour working at the bakery."

But now the focus of the summer of '77 had to change. Henderson had to go to the Caps' training camp in a couple of months. And he had some work to do. Henderson spent the summer trying to get in shape. The Capitals had told Archie they wanted him to weigh in at 207 pounds at training camp and be able to run a mile in five minutes and forty seconds. That would not be a challenge for any NHL pick in the modern era, but this was 1977. And this prospect worked in a factory where he could feast on anything. When the Capitals picked Henderson, he weighed 240 pounds. He had just weeks to lose the weight. So, he embarked on a physical fitness program that consisted of not eating and running behind a Honda. "I just didn't eat. I went to work. I wouldn't eat lunch and I started losing weight. I started running, and I'm not the best runner. I'm not an antelope, let's put it that way. So, here's what I did . . ."

The only personal trainers you would see in the late '70s were old guys at the YMCA with medicine balls. Professional hockey players did not exactly go over the edge in terms of off-season fitness. But Archie Henderson had an edge: his then girlfriend and now wife, Alice. And she had a secret weapon: her yellow Honda Civic.

"We went down by the river in the community that I lived in, and we worked out exactly from start to finish one mile on the odometer of her Honda Civic. Every day after work, I would go down to this area down along the river, and Alice would get in her car and she would drive. And she would drive it at the exact speed so that one mile took five minutes and forty seconds to complete. I would run directly behind the Honda Civic. And I did that every day until

I went to training camp. It goddamn near killed me from the carbon monoxide," howls Henderson.

Next stop was Capitals training camp, held in Hershey, Pennsylvania. Henderson took his spot on the track at the Hershey High School football stadium. He had already weighed in at the required 207 pounds, plus he had done the thirty push-ups and thirty sit-ups the Capitals also required. The only thing he needed to do now was run the mile in five minutes and forty seconds. The only thing that was missing was Alice's Honda Civic. No matter. "I run the mile in exactly five minutes and forty seconds. And as I cross the finish line, I turned to head coach Tom McVie and I go, 'What's next?' I just laughed."

Henderson would not be laughing for long. It turned out that what was next for him was starting his first professional season with the Port Huron Flags of the International Hockey League. And just a few games into this first pro season, Archie Henderson was involved in an on-ice incident that made it into the pages of *Sports Illustrated* for its sheer shocking level of violence. "I can tell you right now, if that happened in today's day and age, they would put the guy in jail, for Christ sakes."

The November 28, 1977, edition of *Sports Illustrated* described the fallout from that night in Port Huron, Michigan, as this: "L'affaire Trognitz has rocked a hockey world still reeling from government investigations into violence as well as a battery of lawsuits and prosecutions by district attorneys for alleged crimes on the ice. Outrageous seemed to be the only word for it."

Trogntiz was Willie Trognitz, at the start of his sixth minor-league season when his Dayton Owls rolled into Port Huron early in the 1977–78 IHL campaign. This was the *Slap Shot* era. Minor-league hockey in the United States could be politely described as a gong show. Trognitz "was an infamous gunslinger in the old IHL," says Henderson. "He played on a line in Toledo called Murder Incorporated. That line had Willie, Dougie Mahood and Paul Tantardini. This was before my time," Henderson adds.

But now, it was Archie Henderson's time. He was a twenty-year-old kid, just a few games into a pro career. Towards the end of the game, there was a faceoff in the Port Huron end. Henderson was on one wing, his tougher-than-nails linemate Gary Rissling, who would go on to accumulate 1,008 penalty minutes in 221 regular-season NHL games, was on the other. "Gary is over against the boards. He gets into a yapping, pushing and shoving matchup with a guy named Rick Dorman, who was a high-penalty-minute guy as well. After the faceoff, all hell breaks loose."

The gloves dropped. Rissling and Dorman went at it. The duo would combine to spend 816 minutes in the box that season, but at this moment they were trading punches, working on at least a combined ten—five minutes each for fighting. As they were going toe to toe, Dayton's John Flesch decided to get in on the action. The handlebar-moustached winger, who was also no stranger to the penalty box, jumped in on Rissling. "Well, I got to come and jump to take care of my little buddy, and I had to fight with John Flesch," says Henderson.

Flesch and Henderson went at it. In the fight, Flesch separated his shoulder, and he let Henderson know it. "He starts screaming, 'My shoulder! My shoulder! My shoulder!' So, I let him go, and as I let him go, I get suckered from the side by Willie Trognitz."

The punch broke Henderson's nose. But that's not what inspired *Sports Illustrated* to write about the incident in its famous pages. It is what happened next, and in the following weeks. Henderson, like any young tough guy in 1977 would, wanted a piece of Trognitz, the guy who'd just smashed his face with a sucker punch. Henderson charged at Trognitz, who at this point was beside his head coach, Nick Polano, by the Dayton bench. Henderson made his way to Trognitz, who did not drop his gloves. "Willie's got his stick in his hand, and he hits me right over the fucking head with his stick, like it was a baseball bat. He hit me right over the head! I go down. I don't remember all this, but they told me that the crowd, they all came down and there were people getting into the fight. It was just a gong show to get me off the ice."

"Port Huron owner Morris Snider called the outbreak the 'worst I've seen in 27 years,'" reported *Sports Illustrated*. "When it was over, Wild Willie had a record 63 minutes in penalties, and Henderson had eight stitches, a broken nose and a slight concussion. He spent the night in a Port Huron hospital."

The IHL suspended Trognitz for life. *Sports Illustrated* picked up the story because, incredibly, just five days after his suspension was announced, Trognitz signed on with the WHA's Cincinnati Stingers. He moved up to a bigger league that gave him a bigger paycheque. Archie Henderson spent the next decade or so of his life in that crazy minor-league world. Sure, things softened up a bit by the mid-1980s, but it was a tough life. There were rewards, though. He played twenty-three games in the NHL—seven for the Washington Capitals, one for the Minnesota North Stars and fifteen for the Hartford Whalers. Henderson's hockey life, though, was mostly spent in the minors.

He was playing in the International League one night when Kalamazoo's Alvin White, the league's penalty leader, a guy who "had a big Fu Manchu moustache and a great big Afro," chased a Zamboni driver around the ice during a pre-game warmup. "The Zamboni driver is going down the middle of the ice and Alvin is swinging his stick at the driver. Now, you got to picture this: The Zamboni driver curls to the right about three feet. He comes back and Alvin hits him again, and he curls to the left. He's going down the ice, trying to clean the ice, and Alvin is running at him and hitting the side of his Zamboni with his stick!"

There were the moves, too. When the time came to move to a new town, Archie and Alice would pack their belongings in the little trailer they hitched to their vehicle and drive to the next town. Henderson led the Hershey Bears with 337 penalty minutes in 1978–79, a mere seventy-nine off the league lead. His reward—well, he didn't like the head coach, Gary Green, and Green didn't like him—was to be loaned out to Fort Worth of the Central League after playing in only eight games with Hershey to start the 1979–80 season. One of his teammates in Fort Worth? Willie Trognitz. It didn't take long for the reunion to get under way. "When I first walked in there and went into the dressing room, it was silent. They sat us across the room from one another. I didn't look at him and he didn't look at me. We had our practice, and then we headed over to Dallas. I'll never forget it. I used to always sit at the front of the bus, three or four rows back, and Willie was sitting in the last row of the bus. I could hear this laughing and I could hear my name, and I knew exactly what was going on. So, I got up and walked down the aisle of the bus, and I grabbed Willie right by the throat and I slammed his head against the back of the bus. And I said, basically, 'If you ever bring it up again, I'm going to kick the snot right out of you.' And it was never brought up again and we ended up being linemates."

Of course they did. They finished one-two for the team lead in penalty minutes as well. Willie had 203. Archie had 199.

Henderson collected story after story. In those days, few of the games were captured on camera. That's what makes it, in a way, so magical. "We all get bigger. We all get better-looking. We all become better players. We're all tougher than we ever were. All the stories get bigger, I think, but they happened. There were all kinds of other things that happened. I keep in touch with Stevie Carlson from the Hanson brothers, and everything that happened in that movie happened."

Henderson retired after the 1987–88 season. He stayed in the game; he always wanted to coach. He coached in Indianapolis, Nashville, Scotland and finally back in Victoria in the WHL. Once his gig in Victoria came to an end, he got an intriguing phone call from a legend in the hockey world, Jack Button, the director of player personnel with the Washington Capitals. Button asked Henderson if he had ever thought about scouting. Henderson replied that he still wanted to coach. Button persisted. "He goes, 'Well, why don't you come to Washington and sit down with David Poile and me? We have a couple of ideas.' And he really didn't say much more."

Henderson took Button up on the offer. He flew to Washington and met with Button and Poile, the Caps' long-time general manager. "David Poile was very, very progressive in those days. I don't want to call the Capitals a small-market team, but they were an underfunded market for the NHL that didn't have a lot of success until David got there. David kept coming up with new things, one of which was to form a pro scouting staff."

A pro scouting staff is a given these days. Every team in the NHL is armed with pro scouts and video and analytics departments. That was not the case when Henderson met with Poile during the 1993–94 season.

"There were only maybe five or six full-time pro scouts in the NHL. Teams didn't really have staff. You have to understand, in those days, let's say you were the general manager of the Toronto

Maple Leafs or the Boston Bruins. Harry Neale was the general manager of the Boston Bruins—this is hypothetical. If Harry's talking to Toronto about a trade, Harry would phone a buddy—say, in Sault Ste. Marie—who is a former player. He would ask him if he would like to go down to Toronto with the wife for the weekend. The Bruins would buy the guy a steak and put them in a room at the Royal York hotel. All they had to do was watch a player, let Harry know what kind of a player he was. That's kind of how it was done."

Poile had bigger plans. He wanted staffers to do this work—and more. "Well, David was getting ahead of it by having guys go on the road and watch games—not amateur scouting, but go to NHL, American and European games."

Before Henderson met with Poile, he was given some advice by Button. "I remember Jack saying to me, 'Archie, when you go in and talk to David, you make sure you tell him exactly how you feel about Phil Housley. Because David loves Phil Housley and wants to trade for him.'"

Button knew what he was doing. He knew that Henderson was not a Housley guy. Button wanted to see if Henderson would stand firm with the GM when it came to a player. "I couldn't stand Phil Housley. And neither could Jack Button. And Jack said, 'Archie, don't bullshit him. Go and tell him exactly what you think.' So, in the interview, sure enough, David brings up Phil Housley and he goes, 'What do you think of Phil Housley?' I said, 'I can't stand him. I don't think you'll win with him.'"

It is a story that still sticks with Henderson and Poile. "David started laughing the other day on the phone. He says, 'I remember that.'"

Henderson's point is you had to stand by what you thought. You didn't always have to agree with your boss. A good debate was all part of the process. He was not going to be a yes man to anyone who hired him. He got the job. He would be one of two pro scouts for the Caps—they split the coverage between the East and West of North America. Pro scouting was an all-new thing. Henderson basically made it up as he went. "We made our own blueprints. In the beginning, I had to figure out how to file reports. I had to figure out which hotels to stay in, which airlines to fly, which cities to fly in to. How do I get into the press box? Stuff like that. You learned as you went."

Pro scouting now is far different than the almost solitary world Henderson stepped into in the mid-1990s. "Now teams have a minimum of five pro scouts on every staff—minimum. They usually have a head guy. They have four scouts who each do a division, but they also have guys who watch only certain players. Some scouts will sit there and watch for eight hours a day and watch players on video. I never went through any of that," Henderson continued. "As I progressed, I ended up becoming director in Edmonton of the pro scouting department, so that sort of stuff I didn't have to go through. Now you got thirty-two teams, so there's five scouts on the team—that's 160 pro scouts in the NHL—and then your video guys are watching stuff back home. It is a completely different game now."

The road became Henderson's home, sometimes for over a month at a time. "I was in the Springfield Marriott so goddamn long, I went and bought a plant," he laughs.

One time during his first year with the Caps, Henderson completed a run of forty straight days on the road. A couple of days after he got home, the phone rang. It was Jack Button, but he didn't want to talk to Archie. He wanted to talk to Archie's wife, Alice.

"Alice gets on the phone, and he goes to her, 'Did Archie take you out for dinner last night?' And Alice says, 'No.' He said, 'Let me talk to Archie.' I pick up the phone and he reamed me out like you can't believe. He said, 'If you ever go on the road again, if you come off the road and you don't take your wife out for dinner on the team,' he said, 'you're going to hear from me.' That's the kind of guy he was. He was a really, really hard guy to work for. He pushed, he pushed, but man, he and David Poile were fantastic."

Henderson would handwrite his reports back then—no fancy computers. He had to make sure his handwriting was neat enough for Poile and Button to read. And if you went out and had a few pops after the game, the last thing you wanted to see when you got back to your hotel room was that red blinking message light.

"If you had a few beers after the game, if you came in at one o'clock and the red light on that phone in your room was blinking, you knew that was Button. And the message would say, 'Phone me back when you come in.' Well, if you came in at one o'clock in the morning and you're phoning him and it's three o'clock in Washington, it didn't go over so well. You know what I mean?"

In those early days with the Caps, Henderson would even help out on the amateur side. He got a call from Button one night. He wanted to get a read on a young defenceman with the IHL's Las Vegas Thunder named Ruslan Salei, who was eligible for the 1996 NHL draft. "The dilemma was Vegas had listed Ruslan Salei at being six foot two, and Jack asked me, "Is this guy six foot two?' I said there was no way this guy was six foot two. Jack said, 'You better be right, because Central Scouting is saying he's six foot two.' I said, 'There's no way he's six foot two.' Jack told me I better be able to prove it."

Archie knew he could prove it. He hit the road and went to Chicago. The Las Vegas Thunder were in town to play the Chicago Wolves. Henderson had something planned, something that no scout would ever be able to do today. Archie knew Bob Strumm, the general manager of the Thunder, and he made that connection work for him.

"I will never forget this," he begins. "I set it up with Bobby Strumm so I could meet with Salei after the game. So, Salei comes out of the dressing room, and I was standing there. Well, you're not allowed to do that now. You're not allowed to hang around the dressing rooms. Ruslan comes out, I shake his hand and I tell him who I am. And I said, 'Let's just go around here. I want you to do something for me.'"

Salei followed the six-foot-six Henderson. Henderson asked Salei to stand up against the wall. "He's looking at me like, 'What the hell are you doing?' I said, 'Stand there.'"

Salei nestled up against the wall. "I pulled a ruler and sewing tape out of my pocket. I put the ruler right on top of his head. I marked the wall, and I measured him with the sewing tape. Ruslan Salei was five foot eleven and a half." Henderson got his man—or, more accurately, his man's measurement for his man.

"I told Jack he was five foot eleven and a half. At the draft table, when Anaheim took him ninth overall, the phone rings."

It was Jack Button. He wasn't at the draft. He was at home, fighting leukemia, but keeping an eye on things. The Caps handed the phone to Archie. "He said, 'You better be right.' I said, 'I don't have to bet. I know how tall he is.' Ruslan went on and had a great career. He's one of the guys who died along with his team entire team, Lokomotiv Yaroslavl, in a Russian plane crash on September 7, 2011."

To this day, Salei is listed on hockeydb.com at six foot two. "But Ruslan was five foot eleven and a half," insists Archie Henderson.

The job of a pro scout is to know the players and the league. Henderson and his scouting partners with the Caps were asked to keep an eye on Adam Oates leading up to the 1997 trade deadline. David Poile wanted his Caps to make a push for the playoffs. The Caps picked up Oates, along with Bill Ranford and Rick Tocchet, for Jason Allison, Anson Carter, Jim Carey and two draft picks on March 1, 1997. "If I had to look back and look at the bigger deals I was involved with, the biggest, without a doubt, was the Adam Oates trade with the Boston Bruins."

It all came together when Poile put the word out to keep an eye on Oates. The Caps put their scouting pieces in place. "We had a guy in the Boston area named Freddy Devereaux. He was, like, a part-time guy and amateur guy doing colleges and stuff. He would go to the games in Boston, and of course, that was a big thing for him to be involved in all the talk because David had him kind of on a special assignment watching Oates. Of course, we knew all the players. David is the one who pulled the trigger."

Landing Tocchet in the deal was another bonus for the Caps. "The excitement of that trade was unbelievable, and of course, getting Toc at the time . . . man, Rick Tocchet was one of the most aggressive, tough, grinding players in the National League at the time. The problem was that the Bruins couldn't get him signed and he wouldn't come immediately to Washington. He held out because he wanted a new contract, and we had to make that trade to try to get us into the playoffs."

The trade did not work, at least in the short term. The Capitals did not make the playoffs in the spring of 1997. After fifteen years with the Caps, David Poile was fired on May 11, 1997. George McPhee became the new GM of the Caps, and that trade worked in the long term. The next season, in the spring of 1998, the Washington Capitals made it to their first Stanley Cup Final. "David was gone, but now you got Adam Oates. We had Peter Bondra. We had Olaf Kolzig in the net. These were all David Poile guys. The pro staff—I don't want to take pats on the back, but we continually started building over the course of that summer again, and then we went to the Stanley Cup Finals for the first time in the history of that franchise."

Henderson would go on to be a pro scout for the Ottawa Senators and the Detroit Red Wings before he ended his career in 2022 as the Edmonton Oilers' director of professional scouting. Words Jack Button said to him early in his career always stuck with him. "Jack Button always told our scouts, 'Don't scout with your ears. Scout with your eyes. But listen to what you hear.'"

That remained a constant for Henderson, even though the game changed on, and especially off, the ice. The way trades are made now has changed. There is the salary cap. There is an analytics department. There is endless video. There are reports saved on computers forever, reports that once upon a time would have been submitted by hand and eventually thrown in the trash. "Nowadays, some scouts, they don't gather information. They do it all analytically. They will talk to the guy in the office about the analytic numbers. Now, do you hear things about players? Yeah. This guy is trying to chase this woman, for example. A good pro scout should hear about that kind of stuff."

You can crunch all the numbers you want, but for Henderson, it was always about being there—at the rink, in the press box—talking and listening, finding out everything he could. "You should go to the press box, and you should bullshit around. The people that know the players best are the other players. They know who's a good player and who's not a good player. That's why general managers now always go to the captains and their leadership group before any kind of a move is made. The players are the ones who know more than anybody else. I can pretend that I know them from sitting up in the press box; the coaches can pretend that they know them from sitting behind the bench; the trainers can pretend to know them from being in the medical rooms; but the players know who the best players are." Henderson almost preaches.

"Do you really think that before [the Oilers] brought in Evander Kane that Ken Holland didn't go to [Connor] McDavid and [Leon] Draisaitl? Do you really think that before the Oilers brought in [Corey] Perry that they didn't go to McDavid and Draisaitl? Or the trade for Mattias Ekholm? Do you really think that? Of course [he did]. Of course, because the players are the ones that know."

How long did it take Henderson to find that out—to know that the players are the ones who really know best? "I knew that right away because I was a former player coming into pro scouting. I knew it right away. In pro scouting," Henderson continues, "what happens is the GMs, they know most of the players because they watch television all the time. Back in my day, in the early days, they didn't have that, not like they do now. So, the GMs are watching games all the time. They have their own opinions, but they rely on what you're thinking to give them a second opinion. A lot of times it is to affirm what they are thinking. And if there are any red flags from your side, then why? Why? Why do you feel this way? What have you heard?"

The other thing that a pro scout needs now, compared to thirty years ago, is flexibility. Careers can last a lot longer now. Players can change. The way they play can evolve. They can go from unneeded in one organization to a prize find for another. "As a pro scout, you really have to be flexible nowadays because players play longer than they used to. Think of examples of players that have changed a lot over their careers. Look at a kid like Michael Bunting."

Bunting was a twenty-five-year-old who had gone up and down

in Arizona's system during his first six pro seasons. He had played twenty-six NHL games when he was signed by Toronto in the summer of 2021. In his first season with the Leafs, he seemingly came out of nowhere, racking up sixty-three points in seventy-nine games. "Well, somebody in that organization saw something that they liked about him and brought him from Phoenix, where he was playing, to Toronto. And a good pro scout, you have to know your own team and what the needs are. Who can fit. How can they fit. But the biggest problem is you can come up with ten names and it will not work because of the salary cap."

There was no salary cap in 1997, when the Caps traded for Adam Oates in that eight-player blockbuster, the type of trade that almost seems impossible these days. The salary cap makes it necessary for a good pro scout to find the right fit, at the right price, for his team. "I laugh," Henderson begins. "In Edmonton, I laugh at even some of the media. They talk about Cody Ceci."

Ceci came to Edmonton because, once upon a time, Adam Larsson, a big right-handed defenceman the Oilers thought was going to be a part of their long-term future, decided he had to leave town. "Larsson didn't let us know until almost the last minute. The reason why was his father dropped dead of a heart attack in the West Edmonton Mall. His mother did not want to come back to Edmonton. There were bad memories. . . . So, Larsson wanted to leave. But he didn't really want to leave, but his family pressure got to him. He lives in Spain during the off-season, and he let the Oilers know it at the last minute. So we were stuck."

Larsson refused the Oilers' attempts to re-sign him and instead signed as a free agent with Seattle on July 21, 2001. Now the Oilers were in a pickle. They needed a right-handed defenceman. "So,

I recommend Cody Ceci," says Henderson, who at the time was the Oilers director of pro scouting. "Now, Cody Ceci, in his first year [with Edmonton], helped our team go to the Western Conference Final, where we lost against Colorado. Everybody was excited about Cody Ceci. Cody Ceci is a number five defenceman. He is not a number one. He's not a number two. He's not a three or four. He's a number five."

But when you are seemingly the replacement for a stud like Larsson, you will take heat from the fans and some in the media, even if your salary—a $3.25 million cap hit, compared to Larsson's $4 million cap hit—gives your team a little wiggle room. "He's played very well in Edmonton, but people want to get rid of him. He is playing for $3.25 million. A guy that plays in your top four, he is usually around $5 million. So, you've got a million, a million and a half to bring in someone like a Corey Perry. They don't get it! And that's where a pro scout has to be on top of his game. Maybe a guy ain't a great player, but he ain't a bad player, but he's playing for decent money."

Over the course of more than thirty years, Archie Henderson watched thousands of hockey games. Did he make mistakes? "A good scout will never admit his mistakes," he said, "but there's not a scout in the world that hasn't made mistakes. I can tell you that right now: Scouts are just like the general managers. There's not a general manager in the world who will admit his mistakes, but there's not one of them who hasn't made a mistake."

Now that it's all over, Henderson can admit at least one error during his scouting days. But can an opinion really be wrong? "You have your opinion on a player like a Phil Housley. That was my opinion. Phil Housley was a great player, a great player. I was wrong on Phil Housley, but that was my opinion!"

It was a hockey adventure that started in his hometown of Calgary, with stops all over North America and even in Scotland. It ended professionally in the summer of 2022. On July 29, 2024, Archie was one of the inaugural inductees on the Western Canada Professional Hockey Scouts Foundation Wall of Honour in Okotoks, Alberta.

CHAPTER 14

Hot Rod

Rod Braceful

Rod Braceful made the climb from minor hockey in Detroit to the NHL and USA Hockey. COURTESY ROD BRACEFUL

You'll never really know when a decision you make will alter your life. For Rod Braceful, that decision came when he was a student at New England College in Concord, New Hampshire. And it wasn't the type of decision that most college kids had to mull over. He wasn't deciding on what to major in. Braceful had to decide on what to do with his life. He was playing hockey at NEC until a lingering ankle injury from his junior days put a premature end to his college hockey career. He was a kid from Detroit who loved playing hockey, but now his playing days were done. He was far away from home. Hockey had been his life. Like most hockey players, he didn't have a regular high school experience. He didn't hang out with his buddies all the time. He missed social functions. He was too busy playing for the Detroit Little Caesars and then junior hockey. Maybe now it was time to put an end to his hockey dreams.

"I had in my head I was just going to finish the school year, transfer back to a school in Michigan, and try to have a regular college experience." He played his final game for NEC during the 2009–10 season.

Rod went to seek advice from someone a lot of kids turn to advice for: his mother. His mother, Barbara, had raised her hockey-loving son as a single mom in Detroit. She knew how passionate he was about the game. "I'll never forget when I talked to my mom," recalls Rod, who made numerous stops on his junior hockey path, playing in Ontario and Massachusetts. "Mom said, 'You like this school. You're comfortable with school. Are you sure you want to just uproot this? You don't know what the next school will be like, especially without hockey.' She brought up some good points. And she encouraged me to go talk to Tom Carroll, who was the coach."

Rod took his mom's advice, and Tom had an idea. "He said, 'It's been a few years since we did it, but a couple years ago, we had a kid stop playing on the team. He was still finishing school, and he was kind of our volunteer assistant.'"

Coach Carroll wanted Rod to take on that role. He wouldn't play for the team, but he could still be part of it as an assistant coach. He could still go to school and be a regular student, and be a part of the coaching staff as well. "He said, 'You can push pucks around and be around the guys, and still be around hockey, as you transition to stop playing and doing the rehab.'"

Rod told the coach he'd take things under consideration, but he had made his decision. "No chance. I had my mind made up like any other stubborn kid."

He was going to go home, but before he made his final decision, he was going to go back to his advisor—his mother. He told her about Carroll's offer to join the coaching staff. "She said, 'That's awesome. I think you should do it.'"

Rod didn't make a decision right away. He applied to Michigan State and got wait-listed. He wouldn't find out until after Christmas whether he had been accepted as a transfer to the school, which meant his choice was simple: take a semester off and sit at home, or take Carroll up on his offer and continue life at New England College. He listened to his mom. He stayed on at NEC. He was going to be a volunteer assistant coach. "And that's kind of how it happened. One thing led to another. It is amazing," Rod says, as he looks back at the start of his hockey career off the ice.

It was the start of his new life. One minute, he was a volunteer assistant coach at NEC, and the next, scouting for the Chicago Blackhawks in the NHL, and now working for USA Hockey as director of player personnel for the US National Team Development Program. Rod's old coach still remembers why he threw out that offer of volunteer coach to the kid with the bum ankle.

"His team-first attitude was awesome, for one," says Carroll, who is still the head coach at NEC. "And he had an infectious personality. He gravitated towards our team. And I thought he was a valuable, contributing member of the team, even though he wasn't able to play. He was a real student of the game and understood the nuances and all the things that went in behind the scenes. And I thought this would be a great opportunity for me to have another set of eyes and another enthusiastic member of our program. It was a good opportunity for him to see the inner workings of a college hockey team. Although it was disappointing for him with his injury, it was certainly a good opportunity for both of us. And I was certainly glad to work with him."

Braceful had fallen in love with the game as a young kid in Detroit. No one in his family had ever played hockey, but like a lot of kids growing up in Motown in the mid-90s, the game caught his eye. The Detroit Red Wings were red hot. They had Steve Yzerman, Nick Lidström, Brendan Shanahan, Sergei Fedorov and Kris Draper. The team won back-to-back Stanley Cups in the springs of 1997 and 1998. "I had a family friend playing and went to go see him play. Then I told my mom I wanted to play. She thought I was just like any other kid. You see something for the first time that's kind of foreign and new, and you say you want to do it, right? But I kept asking her to play, and my godmother told her, 'Just sign him up.'"

Eventually, Rod's godmother took matters into her own hands and signed Rod and his cousin up to play hockey. They started, like a lot of other kids, in a learn-to-skate program. "I was falling in love with the sport. The Red Wings were turned around then at that point. There was a big hockey buzz in the city of Detroit."

And the guys on the Red Wings weren't the only hotshots in town. It turns out that young Braceful was a pretty decent little player himself. He started to climb up the hockey ladder and play on some pretty decent teams. Here's the beauty of his hockey journey: unlike a lot of kids who are constantly preached at and aware of the rep hockey journey, Rod was mostly unaware of it all. "I had fun with hockey because I was hanging out with my buddies, getting experience. That was stuff that I didn't really get to experience in my day-to-day life. I grew up in a single-parent home in Detroit. We weren't poor by any means, but we didn't have a lot. My mom worked two jobs the majority of the time when I played AAA. When I went on road trips, another parent would take me and I got to hang out with my buddies. Hockey was about the experience of having camaraderie with a group and being a part of a team.

"I was impressed that with hockey, it didn't matter where you were from. It didn't matter what school you went to. It didn't matter what clothes you wore. You were part of this team, and once you're a part of this team, you're accepted as a brother. And I think for me, being Black and growing up in Detroit, and then getting out, I realized the more I played high-level hockey that I was a minority. I didn't realize that at the start. For me, it was about being accepted, playing hockey, having the time of my life."

Hockey was fun for Rod. It was a sport that accepted him for who he was. The fact that he was really good at the game and that he could perhaps play college hockey didn't really dawn on him until his sophomore or junior year of high school. Why? Even though it is not as outrageous as it is today, high-level hockey was not cheap. While Rod was having the time of his life, his mom was grinding it out, trying to pay for it. "If hockey was as expensive as it is today, there's no way I would have been able to play. Our team had things like charity golf outings, and we'd sell pizza kits. We had all types of fundraisers. Every year, I would write a letter to find some people who would help me out and sponsor me. But I think it was way easier to get by. The equipment wasn't as expensive. We were using wood sticks."

His mother was always there to help. "One time, it was right when two-piece sticks were coming out, I was using a Montreal wood stick, and I broke a couple. And my mom said, 'We're just going to buy a dozen.' So, she ponied up and bought me twelve sticks. And those things lasted forever."

After his AAA season with the Detroit Little Caesars under-16 team, hockey reality started to hit Braceful. Like a lot of kids in search of a life in the game, hockey took him out of his hometown. He crossed the border and headed north to play Junior A in Chatham, Ontario. That's when the nomadic days began. "As I got into junior hockey, I got traded. I played for a bunch of teams. I kind of bounced all around. But I had a good experience, and now that I look back on it, I realize how fortunate I am. I know there's a ton of people that didn't have good experiences, and sometimes there's a little bit of reminders—and I don't want to call it PTSD, but there's things that trigger them—and unfortunately, they didn't have a good experience. My whole time wasn't perfect, but for the most part I had a really good time. Some of my best friends are people that I met in hockey—I wouldn't know them, otherwise."

That junior experience of going from team to team is perhaps why Barbara encouraged her son to hang on at NEC. And he did. But after that time on Tom Carroll's staff, Rod started bouncing around again. He was continuing his climb up the hockey ranks. After serving on Carroll's staff, Rod went back to Detroit to help out with an under-14 team. The next season, he coached the under-15 and under-16 teams and a select travel squad. The following year, he was an assistant coach on the Little Caesars under-16 team, he started to scout for the United States Hockey League's Sioux Falls Stampede, and he had his select travel teams as well. By the 2017–18 season, Rod was helping coach a couple of youth teams as well as serving as head scout of the Muskegon Lumberjacks. He was a busy man, a man whose life was now full time in hockey. "I think that when you embrace the journey and you learn from it, it makes you a better person. You understand there are no shortcuts."

And while he was on this journey, Rod kept believing. Even if he was just coaching kids, he constantly believed he was going to move up the hockey ladder. "I was running a spring and summer program with All-Star tournament teams, and I was running camps, and we had really good twelve- or thirteen-year-olds. And I remember thinking I can coach in the USHL. I can scout in the USHL. I can be a GM in the USHL. I can get the best young kids to come play in the tournament for me. And we beat everybody. I remember thinking, *At some point, this is going to happen for me. Maybe now this might not be my time.*"

Braceful kept coaching. And he kept applying for jobs at higher levels. Rejection happened. "I never got discouraged about not getting jobs. I never once thought, *I'm done with this.* I almost made a promise to myself that if the hockey-player side of me couldn't make it to the NHL, I could make it anyway. Deep down inside of myself, I knew I was really good at what I was doing [coaching and scouting]. I told myself I'm going to make it to the NHL in some capacity."

Braceful's persistence finally paid off. The NHL didn't come calling for the 2018–19 season, but USA Hockey did. USA Hockey revolutionized hockey development in America when it launched the US National Team Development Program in 1996. It has become a breeding ground for the best young American players in the game. Instead of having the top talent scattered around the country, the USA now has a home base—players practise and play on teams together in Plymouth, Michigan. In 2018, Rod was hired as the assistant director of player personnel for the program. The translation of that title is basically "scout, player evaluator." (Essentially, he was the assistant GM.) Rod was now helping to select the best juniors in the US. That first season with the team now reads like a who's who of young superstars: Cole Caufield, Matty Beniers, Jack Hughes, Trevor Zegras.

Unlike NHL scouting, where you are projecting what a player's game might be like three to five years down the road, Rod had to project for right now, for the US program. What's the biggest difference between scouting for right now, as opposed to the future? "That's a great question. One, you have to be honest with yourself and be organized and understand you have to make a decision—who is the best fit for the immediate future? The hardest part of the job, then and now, is the fact that you're not naive. There's a ton of good players, but we're only selecting twenty-two or twenty-three for our team.

"That's the hard part of the job for me. Every weekend, every day, I'm in the rink and I see players who I know are going to be good players, but they may not be ready, at least for our timeline to make our team."

Braceful continued, "It's kind of a backhanded compliment. I see some really good players who may not be ready for our program at the moment. As I say, you have to be honest with yourself, and understand what our program is about and try to find the best puzzle piece, because you're creating a chart of who's going to come into your program and excel. Who can soak up the resources? Who can handle it? Because our program is hard. Who is going to use our program as a platform to take off? And that's really what we're looking for. We need players who are going to be able to come into a super-competitive environment full of top players. It's a real test. For a lot of these kids, it is the first time where they are not the alpha or the best player on the ice.

"That's the second part of the answer to your question: the kids themselves," said Braceful. "Just how are they going to handle that? That is, not being the best player on the ice. Are they going to be able to continue to be who they are? Or is it going to derail them because they've never handled adversity like this before?"

That's just the nature of the game. The higher you climb on hockey's ladder, the more challenging the game will, or at least should, become. The program Rod works for brings in the best players from around the country. The players are now up against every other kid who was the best in his town or state. "I think at USA Hockey as a whole, we're super happy that we can continue to put markers in for kids to chase their dream and grow the game. At one point, American kids dreamt of just playing college hockey. If you were lucky enough to be good in college, then you could play pro. But I think as the game has grown and as the ADM [American Development Model] model has been implemented, you now have kids dreaming to play for the national team and then be drafted high and going on to play in the NHL. I think we've changed the narrative a bit. And these kids aren't afraid to dream."

The dream has changed. It's no longer just a kids from a few states dreaming of landing a college scholarship. The dream is now shared by kids all over the USA. And for most, a scholarship to an NCAA school is no longer the end goal. It is, for most, just the start of the dream now. "American hockey used to be Massachusetts, Michigan, Minnesota. Those kids weren't shocked to have success in hockey. But now we have a guy like Auston Matthews, a player who is of [Mexican] descent, coming from Arizona can be the number one overall pick in the NHL draft is remarkable. And he came through the national team: that shows how much growth has happened in this game in the United States."

The program has also bucked some traditional hockey trends. Size, for one, is not all that matters for a lot of players in the program. Take Montreal Canadiens defenceman Lane Hutson. The baby-faced blueliner from Holland, Michigan, is listed at five foot ten and 162 pounds. Rod first saw Hutson when he was even smaller. A defenceman like that, just a few years ago, would have been passed over almost immediately. "When I first saw Lane Hutson, and I'll never forget this, I told our scouting staff, 'I don't know if he'll ever play in the National Hockey League.' But this kid's a winner. And this kid is a kid you want in your program. Because he just drives winning qualities. There's no harder worker. He handles his business like a gentleman. He's a quiet leader. It's a cliché, but he really does lead by example. When it comes to his hockey skills, it's like he is a video game character. It's impressive what he can do. And I remember thinking—and I'm not telling you this just to tell you this, it's so unfortunate what happened with Johnny Gaudreau [who was killed when a car hit him and his brother Matthew while they were bicycling in the summer of 2024], but I remember talking to Lane. And Lane was telling me his favourite player was Patrick Kane. Kane is a forward, but Lane is a defenceman. And I remember thinking Lane is the defenceman version of Johnny Gaudreau because of the fast twitch, the hesitation, the skating, the way he's able to cut back and weave and turn on a dime. In my mind, Lane is Johnny Gaudreau, but he's playing defence. I think that when you have a kid like Lane, and you get him in an environment where he continues to take strides because he wants to play in the NHL, and he won't be denied until he does it, that shows the leaps and bounds of USA Hockey."

After three years of working with USA Hockey, Rod's dream finally came true. He was hired to scout for the Chicago Blackhawks. He had made it to the NHL.

The first person he called? "My mom. I owe so much to my mom. She made a lot of sacrifices. I think that deep down with her, hockey was able to keep me out of trouble, keep me focused and keep me chasing something. Whether it was attainable or not, I think she thought that in my younger years, it was good to keep me on a path of being positive and not get caught up in other things. Once I got older, I think she was fine and happy and content with whatever I did for work. No matter the industry. When I told her that I was going all in on hockey and working in hockey, she was happy. But she was just happy that I was happy. And I think that making it to the NHL, being able to work in the NHL, was a special moment just to show that all the sacrifices and all the things that she did for me paid off."

Rod got right into the business of scouting, bringing that experience from USA Hockey to the Blackhawks. What did he bring from the program? "I think it was the nuances of understanding the mindset of the younger players and how this generation has changed. The game hasn't changed, but the people have. We had Rob Facca [Chicago's head scout] on staff, who worked in college hockey. He adheres to some of those same opinions, because in college hockey, you have to recruit. And in recruiting, you need to know who the people are, what makes them tick, how they handle themselves and how people are different. And then maybe that paints a story that when you go see a player play, and they play a certain way, maybe it's their personality. Maybe it's how they conduct themselves. Maybe the player is a coach pleaser. They're just going to play like this because that's what's being asked of them wherever they play. The big thing for us is just getting to know the people as well as getting to know the player. Because as a scout, your eyes can tell you, and you have your markers, you know what you like and what you don't like. That's the beauty of scouting. And we all see it differently. That's why there's a scouting staff. If it was so easy that one person can do it, well, there would just be one guy. And the reason that we scout in the NHL is because it takes a village. People see players differently. We're not all going to see the same person the same way."

Rod had his "Welcome to the NHL" moment at the 2022 draft in Montreal. "Marty St. Louis got onstage. He had just been added as a coach there prior to that season. And they did a tribute, and the fans are going nuts. And Kent Hughes is the GM of Montreal. I had met Kent because he was an agent and he had players in our program and his son played in our program. There was a little bit of surrealness when I was sitting on the draft floor. I kind of saw how far I had come. I could feel it. I never really thought about how far I had come until that moment. Before that moment I thought, *I'm going to work really hard and be a good person and this is all going to work out.* At its best, what I do for a living doesn't feel like a job. That's all I was focused on until that point. But I would say that in Montreal, on the draft floor, was a surreal moment."

The day got better. Rod walked up on the stage with the Blackhawks brass when they were ready to make the thirteenth-overall pick. Blackhawks general manager Kyle Davidson stepped to the microphone and announced Chicago's pick. "The Chicago Blackhawks are proud to select, from the United States National Development Team, Frank Nazar."

The Blackhawks had just drafted one of the players Rod had chosen for the US program a couple of years earlier. Nazar had gone through the same program with Rod, and now he was about to join him on the same stage. "I recruited Frank [to the USNDT], and Frank was a high-level midget player coming out of Detroit. He was on that 2004 [birth year] team, and that 2004 team only had two players from Michigan. The London Knights drafted Frank, and they were all over Frank [to go to the OHL], and we got Frank to come into our program for two years. The icing on the cake was being on that stage in the first round and being able to be a part of our staff drafting him. It was another surreal moment."

Nazar did what all first-rounders do when they are in the venue when drafted. He hugged his friends and family, walked to the stage, shook hands with NHL commissioner Gary Bettman, and put on his new team's hockey sweater and a hat. He then made his way to the Blackhawks staff who were on the stage, for his draft day photo. The first person from the Blackhawks to meet Nazar was Rod Braceful. There was only one thing for Rod to say to the kid. "I said, 'Welcome to the National Hockey League.'

"Frank scored a goal in his first NHL game. I wasn't able to get to Chicago for the game, but I watched it and he scored. This is one of those things where you don't know how much impact you have on some of these players and their families . . . but you're helping them chase their dreams."

Rod didn't stick around the NHL for long. He was only with Chicago for two seasons. It may seem to some like a step back down the ladder, but Rod went back to the US National Team Development Program, this time as the director of player personnel. Perhaps instead of a step back, it was a step up. "I think so. I think coming back to the USA program, where I'm able to be in a director role, be able to help out, and help with some of our international teams, whether it's the World Juniors, or the Hlinka [the Hlinka Gretzky Cup, for the world under-18 championship], or the Five Nations is a big step up for me. I think those are opportunities we didn't have in the past.

And I also think that, for me, it's getting to know as many players as possible and how to organize and run teams.

"It's pretty special. For me, it's learning something, every day. The moment you stop learning, that's the moment you know you're in the wrong industry. I was able to come back here and continue to learn, and continue to round out my experiences and get better."

The goal for Rod is to get back to the NHL. And eventually, he'd like a major seat at the table. "Hopefully, one day when I do make it back to the NHL, I'm just that much better, and more equipped to be able to help an organization.

"I want to be a general manager, and I know there's steps to that. That would be my dream job."

And if Rod makes it to the NHL as a GM, he would be following in the footsteps of one of his friends. Mike Grier, just like Rod, was a Black kid who grew up in a predominately white game. Grier is now the GM of the San Jose Sharks. Braceful is part of a nonprofit group called Next Gen, along with Grier, former NHLer Bryce Salvador and Florida assistant GM Brett Peterson. "We got together at the outset of COVID. We wanted to do a hockey camp, but there were all the regulations and whatnot. So, we had a little bit of a team we put together for a tournament. It was a summer tournament, and they won the championship. It was the Beantown Classic. We were eating, and we were having a coffee and laughing. And at that time, Brett Peterson was an agent and advisor. Mike Grier was just a loving dad. He took a little bit of a step back from hockey to be with his family. He was helping out with his kids in hockey. And Bryce Salvador was doing the same, helping out with some younger youth stuff in New Jersey. And he had done some stuff on TV with the Devils and MSG Networks.

"And then you fast-forward a couple years later, I ended up

getting a job with the Blackhawks, Brett Peterson became assistant GM in Florida, and Mike became a GM in San Jose. And I just think about how we were all hanging out, talking, having lunch and smiling, and talking about what we can do so that when our kids are our age, hopefully they get the chance to do this and talk about it. Two years later . . . you have a GM, an assistant GM, and I'm at USNT. It's pretty remarkable."

It is remarkable for four friends to climb a ladder like that. But in order for the climb to continue, the work has to continue for Rod Braceful. He wants to make it back to the NHL, and so do the kids in his program. He now knows what both levels of the game are after. There are thirty-two teams in the NHL, trying to put together a puzzle. And for any good scout, the key is seeing and believing what others may not see or believe when they look at a player and try to put a puzzle for a team together. "I remember telling people that Brock Faber is a first-round pick. I remember getting laughed at. Other scouts told me, 'You're a regional scout, we get it, you love him, but you see him every day. Brock Faber . . . come on, he's below six feet. He's not a first-round pick.' And I told them, 'What is it that he doesn't have besides his height? Take Lane Hutson: What is it that he doesn't have beside his height?' A player works out or he doesn't. If they can think the game, if they can skate, if they can manage the puck, who cares about his height? Just what are you looking for? Brock Faber is a big-time player. He'll be playing in the National Hockey League for twenty years, no doubt about it."

Faber was picked forty-fifth overall by the LA Kings in 2020. In 2023–24 he played in his first full NHL season, scoring forty-seven points in eighty-two games for the Minnesota Wild. "The game is so fast now. So fast. If guys can skate and play within the game, and they have sense and they have skill and the ability to play to an identity, then thirty-two teams will want that player. And that's what we're trying to prepare our players for coming out of our program.

"Players have to play to an identity because it's always going to change. I look at playoff hockey, or look at a kid who comes into the NHL, whether it's from college, or whether it's a call-up from the American League . . . a kid from the American League can get called up, a kid who has more than a point a game and is on the power play of his AHL team. A call-up from the AHL. Where does he play in the NHL? Most likely on the third line. They will play ten or twelve minutes. Which means as a player, you have to adapt. You have to adjust. You have to have a certain identity. But if you know a kid can know his worth and play a certain identity, then when you're able to adapt to change . . . you're able to still have success.

"The game is super fast," he continued, "and it's super skilled, but a skill is having an identity. And can you believe into that identity, and can you adapt as a player? Because you can be the best player on a middle-tier team, but when you go to the top team, can you mesh well and be a middle-of-the-pack player, and help that team win?"

Rod is on a roll, talking hockey, spewing out scouting knowledge that he has acquired over years in the game, on a unique path, one that began when his playing days ended and his mother told him to accept that offer from his college hockey coach to join him on his staff.

"I'm happy for Rod," says his old coach, Tom Carroll. "I never thought that this would be what would happen. I thought that the coaching chance would be good for him and good for our team. I'm so thrilled for him; it's great, and everybody wants to see their players and students have an impact or have success. And he's paid it forward; maybe he's seen a diamond in the rough, a player other scouts have overlooked, and has provided an opportunity for somebody else."

"Hockey literally changed my life," says Rod. "I'm working in hockey. I'm Black, from Detroit, went to public school. I didn't think I would be working in hockey full time as my job. It makes me feel like a child sometimes. I kind of laugh at it, actually."

CHAPTER 15

The Most Interesting Scout in the World

Paul Henry

Hockey has taken Paul Henry all around the globe. Here he is on a European scouting trip with Halifax Mooseheads general manager Cam Russell (middle) and the legendary Pierre Pagé (right). COURTESY CAM RUSSELL

"You have to meet Paul in person," says Halifax Mooseheads general manager Cam Russell. "You can't interview him on the phone. You have to meet Paul in person."

For years, the Halifax Mooseheads have had a pipeline to Europe. They have unearthed and stolen players from all over the continent—some that no other teams had on their radar. The secret to the Mooseheads' European success, according to Russell, is one of the most genuine people you will ever meet. He is a man who is thirsty for life. He is a man who has worked with men serving life sentences at the maximum-security Millhaven Institution. "What's that one song from The Tragically Hip, '38 Years Old'? . . . I told him about that song, and he said, 'No, there were fifteen, not twelve [escaped convicts], and one of the escaped criminals came back because the mosquitoes were too thick.' He's priceless, this guy. You could write a book on Paul alone," says Russell.

Yes, Paul Henry worked behind bars. He is a man who ran a halfway house. He is a man who would visit his prisoners years later. He is a man with a master's in psychology from the University of Guelph. If the Dos Equis man is the most interesting man in some fictional beer advertising world, then Paul Henry is the most interesting man in the scouting world.

Russell and Henry have made several trips to Europe together, renting cars and staying in hotels, scouting and sharing stories. "Not until you really sit down with somebody like that and spend some time and get to know Paul—not just in hockey, but in life—do you appreciate someone like him," says Cam Russell. "Everyone is in a hurry nowadays. When you meet people and you don't really give them the time to get to know them. Well, when you sit down with a guy like Paul Henry and you talk to him and you go through his history and everything he's done and who he has worked for, the players that he has drafted, it's incredible. You can throw the name of any player out and he will tell you his birthday, who he played junior for, where he played his minor hockey. Paul is a walking encyclopedia."

I ask Cam for Paul's number, and he is happy to pass it along.

The search for Paul Henry ended, rather surprisingly, at Paul Patskou's hockey alumni luncheon in Toronto. A friendly face walked up and introduced himself to me, and before I could tell him how absolutely thrilled I was to randomly run into him, he blurted out, "You didn't do George Pelawa justice in your last book."

First off, I was honoured that a hockey man like Henry had read my last book, *Ken Reid's Hometown Hockey Heroes*. And secondly, Paul was right. How could I do justice to the Paul Bunyan of hockey? I had never seen the phenom who was George Pelawa, but of course Paul Henry had. He was scouting for the New York Rangers in the winter and spring of 1986. That's when Pelawa, a hulking six-foot-three, 230-pound forward, came out of nowhere to dominate the Minnesota high school hockey scene. He was, physically at least, a man among boys. "Impact player," Henry begins. "An impact human being. And he had an impact interview. There has never been one before. There has never been once since. That would be my only way of describing George Pelawa."

Then, as if he were still in the rink these thirty-eight years later, Henry begins to describe what he saw on the ice from Mr. Hockey Minnesota in 1986. "It was a big tournament in Boston, a state showcase. I believe it was in Lowell. We were watching Minnesota. I don't remember who they were playing, but they were down 10–3, and George went to work and they won, 11–10."

A couple of months after that tournament, Henry was part of the Rangers brass who interviewed Pelawa as the 1986 draft approached.

The Rangers had the ninth pick in the first round, but they didn't take Pelawa with that pick. They took future Hall of Famer Brian Leetch. For the record, Henry had wanted the Rangers to take Adam Graves at number four. "In '86 with the New York Rangers, there were two American scouts and me, and I was fighting for a guy by the name of Adam Graves who I had fourth overall. I'd seen him eighteen times. I fought tooth and nail for Graves for three weeks. I lost the fight. But the guy who we picked was Brian Leetch."

Henry let Graves and Leetch in on the scouting secret years later, "at Henry Graves' funeral after he died at the age of fifty-seven. There was Brian and Adam in their suits, and I told them that story. I told them that story and how it worked out. They were both members of the '94 New York Rangers.

"We were a team when we picked," Henry continued. "It was a consensus. I remember Adam's coach, Bill Gunter, from the Toronto Young Nats. He was about to kill me for not picking Adam. I wanted Adam. And Adam didn't go until twenty-two, to Detroit. And Bill Gunter was about to kill me at the draft. I can still feel his rage."

Now back to Pelawa, who went a few picks before Graves and a few picks after Leetch. Pelawa was an off-the-board kid. He didn't score a goal in his first year of high school hockey at Bemidji High. Two years later, he was sitting in front of Paul Henry and the New York Rangers brain trust for his pre-draft interview. The kid was a giant. He'd scored twenty-nine goals and added twenty-four assists for Bemidji High during his senior year. The kid was committed to go to the University of North Dakota on a full hockey scholarship in the fall. The word that keeps popping up here is *kid*. Pelawa had just turned eighteen a few months earlier. Two years before he met with Henry and the Rangers, the NHL wasn't even a dream. Now it was becoming more and more like a reality.

In 1986, draft-eligible kids weren't polished as they are today, especially ones from the woods of Minnesota. "George just oozed with charisma," Henry says in amazement. "How many people ooze with charisma? We asked George, 'Who's your favourite team?' He said, 'The Calgary Flames!' No one could believe his answer, of course. He's supposed to say the New York Rangers! Then we asked him, 'What are your interests?' He said, 'Hockey, booze and broads. In that order!'" Big George wasn't trying to be polished, he wasn't trying to be anything but who he was. "His honesty, and his raw, raw, raw charisma and character," Henry says of what stood out to him about George that day. "He was just a really unique human being."

The Calgary Flames selected Pelawa with the sixteenth pick. The draft took place on June 21. George Pelawa died in a car accident on August 20, 1986. The news of his death still sticks with Paul Henry. "I was sitting at the Red and White store in Norland, Ontario. I bought the paper and opened it up. I saw the news and I sat there in stunned silence for a good hour. I was overwhelmed. I felt the same sadness years later—I was in the exact same stunned silence when Princess Diana died."

Henry continues, "George could've been . . ." He struggled for the words. "I watched Tom Wilson [of the Washington Capitals] right there in that rink, that rink right there. And it wasn't even close. George, he was a wrecking ball, but he also had skill and talent." Wilson has made a living as a tough physical player. He is a Stanley Cup champion.

George Pelawa is just one of the thousands of young players Paul Henry has watched over the years. He is an evaluator of talent, and so much more. The "so much more" part makes a lot of sense when you consider his background.

Let's go back to jail. "I was the only psychologist in the max security prison Kingston Penn," says Henry. Being a hockey guy—he grew up and went to grade school with Howie and Dave Draper—he naturally stuck with the game, even during his chosen time behind bars. "I played hockey every night on the outdoor rink with the boys in prison."

When the snow cleared, though, and the ice disappeared, it seems the players got a little antsy and wanted a change of scenery. "That summer, the guy I called the Candyman orchestrated the largest escape in maximum-security history. Fifteen guys escaped. One guy came back because the mosquitoes were so bad. The guy was doing twenty years for manslaughter, but he decided to come back because the mosquitoes were so bad."

ONTARIO'S BIGGEST PRISON BREAK, the headline screamed on the cover of the July 11, 1972, edition of the *Toronto Star*, 14 PRISONERS BREAK OUT OF MAXIMUM SECURITY JAIL. But now we know it was fifteen, but one guy came back because of the bugs.

So, what can working among over five hundred inmates at Canada's most notorious maximum-security prison teach a guy? What can a guy take from that experience years later when he is a hockey scout? What did Paul Henry learn from working in prison that applies to hockey? "Toughness. Absolutely, I learned more in my time at Kingston Pen than in any classroom. I learned more from those guys. They taught me more than I ever learned from everybody. They all came from absolutely horseshit backgrounds. It was just emotional toughness. It was just a really special learning experience."

Just like the prisoners, Henry had to ease into life on the outside as well. "I went from there to running a halfway house for three and a half years, and I hired all my buddies."

This leads to yet another story. "In fact, I hired a guy named Kevin O'Shea. His dad, Daniel O'Shea, was the second-best junior in the country after Bobby Orr. Danny's date when he played for the Minnesota North Stars was Loni Anderson. She was the star of *WKRP in Cincinnati*. She married Burt Reynolds."

Paul knew all about Danny's hockey career. He knew that he was a stud blueliner for the Peterborough Petes and Oshawa Generals before he joined the Canadian National Team. And he knew that he went on to average over almost half a point a game on the blue line during his time in the NHL. But he didn't know about Loni until years later. Even the best scouts don't know everything, "I've been best friends with Danny since we were sixteen, but he never told me he dated Loni Anderson."

Oh yeah, back to the halfway house. Just like Millhaven, it came with its share of adventures. "One of the guys was fifty-eight years old. He spent twenty-two years on a cellblock with the Boston Strangler. He came after me three weeks in a row with a sawed-off shotgun."

Henry survived that one, too, and then he eventually got the call. A few years later, former NHL goalie Wayne Thomas was on the phone and he wanted to talk to Paul Henry. "Actually, my story starts with Wayne Thomas. He was the assistant coach of the New York Rangers, and they had a guy who had three goals and three assists in twenty-five games. Wayne told [head coach] Herb Brooks that I could help him. So, I had a session with the guy at the press club in Toronto. He went out and scored four goals the next game, and two the game after that. He got player of the week, and I've been in hockey ever since. I can't tell you who the guy is."

A little research online could tell you who the player was, but let's respect the psychologist-patient relationship. That one chat started it all for Paul Henry. Soon enough, he joined the Rangers staff. "I basically worked for the Rangers from '82 to '86. They paid me 50 percent psychology and 50 percent scouting," he chuckles.

As soon as Henry starts talking about the Rangers, he brings up Herb Brooks, who led Team USA to gold at the 1980 Olympics. The world knows that game and that conquest as the Miracle on Ice.

Henry got a call one day from Rangers general manager Craig Patrick. He wanted Henry to come down and have a chat with Mike Allison. Allison's career had gotten off to an incredible start. In his rookie season of 1980–81, he scored twenty-six goals and thirty-eight assists in seventy-five games. He was one of the top scorers on the team under head coach Fred Shero. Brooks took over the next year, Allison's numbers went down, and he even ended up spending some time in the minors during his second and third pro seasons. "Craig calls me and says, 'Get down here. Mike Allison needs to see you.' So, I fly into New York and Herbie picks me up."

Henry soon discovered the problem the old-school Brooks had with Allison. "Herb has a thirty-minute rant about Mike Allison, the first guy to wear an earring in the National Hockey League. Herb was just rattled beyond belief. So, anyway, I got half an hour of this rant from Herb."

All Henry could do was listen. "And I'd known Mike. And I love Mike to this day, first pick overall in the OHL draft, a Fort Frances guy. Anyway, I see Mike the next day and he has his earring in. I say, 'Mike, I like your earring, but not half as much as your perm,'" Henry laughs. Problem solved.

One night, Henry was scouting in Lake Placid, New York. Being at the site of the Miracle, he decided to give the man behind the Miracle a call. Paul picked up the phone and dialed. But Herb didn't answer—Herb's wife, Patti, did. "Patti was one of the most beautiful women ever and had character of the highest order. I got talking to her for three minutes, and she said, 'Where are you?' I said, 'I'm overlooking the site of your husband's greatest conquest!'

"The line went dead. There was silence, until Pattie blurted, 'Where are you? In my bedroom?'"

Henry loved that zinger. He says Herb loved it, too. "In fact, the last time I saw him alive was March 3, 2003, and he told that story to 1,200 people when he was a guest speaker at the USHL banquet. And the last time I talked to Herb, he was on the set of [the movie] *Miracle*. And he told me that Patti said that if Kevin Costner was going to play him, then Patti was going to play herself."

Herb Brooks died in a car accident on August 11, 2003, in Minnesota. *Miracle* was released on February 6, 2004. At the end of the film, before the credits rolled, a note on the screen read, "This film is dedicated to the memory of Herb Brooks, who died shortly following principal photography. He never saw it. He lived it."

"At the cemetery, I told Herb's wife what he said about Kevin Costner the last time I talked to him. She said, 'Nah, it was George Clooney.'"

Henry almost had his own version of the Miracle on Ice. This one would have taken place in Lillehammer, Norway. Henry was working for the St. Louis Blues when he got a call one day. He was asked to help put together Team Canada for the 1994 Olympics—the Games were just eighteen months away. Ron Caron, the man in charge of the Blues, let him go and take on the Olympic challenge. "I got the longest leave of absence in history. I took the job. I signed every guy except for Petr Nedvěd."

So, how do you find players—over the course of their careers, or even over the course of eighteen months? "I mean, basically players find me. I don't find players. They find me."

One player who was a shoo-in for that Olympic team was Paul Kariya. Henry was at Kariya's first-ever college hockey game, at the Alfond Arena on the campus of the University of Maine in the fall of 1992. Kariya was about to turn the college hockey world upside down. Less than a week after he turned eighteen, he played in the first game of the Black Bears' historic 42–1–2 season.

"Two guys every year pull me out of my seat. It was Paul's first college game ever. Maine 9, Providence College 2. Paul Kariya—two goals, two assists. I went out for breakfast with him the next day and commended him on his performance. He said, 'No, it was one [goal] and one [assist].' Two guys had stolen one and one on him, and he couldn't care less. Six months later, I'm at Milwaukee at the national final. Paul's rookie of the year. He's the Hobey Baker [Award, for the top men's collegiate hockey player] winner and he's a national champion. And he has a hundred points and he couldn't care less about the two points that were stolen off him. That's just unique and special."

Kariya had the Olympics in his blood. At least, he had the quest to be an Olympian in his blood. "His dad, Tetsuhiko Kariya, hung with the '68 Olympians at the University of British Columbia. They were all advocates of Father David Bauer [who formed Canada's first-ever national team], like me. Kariya's father was a national-level rugby guy whose best friends were all hockey players. So, Tetsuhiko Kariya fell in love with hockey. Paul's dad wasn't going to allow him to play pro until he got the Olympic experience because he was so enamoured with his buddies in '68 and how classy the Olympians were."

So, Kariya was easy. As for the rest of the roster, it took a lot of work and a lot of miles. "I wanted everybody in the country to be proud of that team. I got a brand-new car every twenty-eight thousand miles from Thrifty. And I went through seven of them putting that team together."

Adrian Aucoin was a big defenceman who spent the 1991–92 season playing for his legendary coach, Jack Parker, at Boston

University. But that was the only one he spent with the Terriers. Paul Henry got him for Lillehammer. "It took me seven visits to his house before he said yes. Jackie Parker threatened me for stealing him. He said he'd never make it. And Jackie apologized six months later when Adrian won a silver medal. Jackie won a national title with Adrian's class in 1995, so he apologized with threatening me with death for stealing Adrian Aucoin."

Todd Warriner was just nineteen years old when he joined the national team in the fall of 1993. The fourth-overall pick in the 1992 NHL Entry Draft, Warriner failed to make the Quebec Nordiques out of training camp. Quebec suggested the national team to him and another young Nordiques prospect, Dwayne Norris, who didn't make the NHL cut that fall. Warriner says he just kind of tagged along with Norris, but once he was in, he was in. "We both went together from Quebec," Warriner says. "So, I know in his recruiting of Dwayne Norris, I probably came up. But, you know, once you're on the team, you're part of Paul's family. I think for the rest of your life, you're going to hear from Paul Henry. You know what I mean?

"At the 2016 Memorial Cup in Halifax, [hockey broadcaster] Jeff Marek and I walked into the Halifax Civic Centre, and there was Paul. I didn't even know he was working for the Mooseheads. I hadn't seen him in fifteen years. So, he tells me a story about running into one of my ex-girlfriends in Haliburton [Ontario] while escorting prisoners from Kingston. He made all us guys on the Olympic team feel like we were perennial All-Stars. He would come up to you after a game where maybe you were minus-4 and didn't score and you had no shots, and he'd say, 'Oh, you were the best player.' You just can't forget him."

And while he was with national team prepping for the Olympics, Warriner would hear the murmurs about Paul Henry and his cross-continent adventures in his Thrifty rental car. The national team was struggling through the fall and early winter leading up to the 1994 Olympics. And behind the scenes, Henry was still doing this thing.

"You know, it's funny," Warriner says. "I can remember [sports psychologist] Cal Botterill saying something to the effect of 'You know, Paul's been on the road for four days.' Cal would come and speak to us. Cal alluded to the fact that Paul was out there, driving across Canada. We all knew what Paul did, but he never showed the effects of it. Paul was immune to sleep. He didn't need sleep."

Henry got another kid out of the NCAA as well, a late bloomer because of his top-notch golf game who went on to play in eleven highly respectable NHL seasons. Brian Savage had two goals and two assists in eight games in Lillehammer. "Savage didn't play hockey for two years because he was too busy golfing. He was the third-best [golfer] in the country after Mike Weir and Mike Weir's caddie. Brian did not play hockey at fifteen or sixteen."

With his team set, Canada got hot at the perfect time. When it was time to face off at Lillehammer, the team Henry put together was playing some pretty decent hockey. They finished the preliminary round second in their group with a 3–1–1 record. The quarterfinal worked out perfectly, with Paul Kariya scoring in overtime in a 3–2 win over the Czechs. That was followed by a 5–3 semifinal win over Finland. And then, Sweden in a gold medal showdown.

As you may know, Canada lost in the gold medal game on Peter Forsberg's shootout winner. Forsberg went in and put a one-handed deke on Corey Hirsch. The goal was so famous in Sweden that it was commemorated on a stamp. "It's not the way you solve a gold medal game—a shootout," Paul shakes his head, his voice still stinging from the result.

Henry, naturally, can still recall the minutiae of the game. "Todd Warriner did not play in the gold medal game. He was hurt with a knee injury. He was on the second line with Brian Savage and Dwayne Norris."

Canada took a 2–1 lead with 8:17 to go in regulation on an unassisted goal by Derek Mayer. "Derek Mayer from Rossland, BC—same as [downhill skiing champion] Nancy Greene—scored [what seemed to be] the game-winning goal and was a national hero for eight minutes."

Mayer would have been a national hero, except Sweden tied it with 1:49 to go. Then, after a scoreless ten minutes of overtime, there was a fourteen-player shootout. "Still, every time I see Forsberg, I give him shit and he says, 'Get over it.' I saw him last two years ago and I told him, 'I'm still not over it, Peter.'

"I've never been in anything comparable, and it is by far my career highlight."

After the Olympics, Paul Henry joined the Florida Panthers, where the scouting and the collection of stories continued. "I remember one day when I was working in Florida," Henry begins, the words flowing from his encyclopedic hockey brain with ease.

This story involves one of the greatest defencemen to ever play the game—a tall, long, raw kid from Slovakia who was the one that got away.

"I went with our great Czech scout Pavel Routa [to check out Zdeno Chára], and he absolutely loved and adored Zdeno Chára. Routa took me to five games that day. And the day before, he took me to Bratislava to see Stanislav Gron or Tomáš Gron. They were brothers. But the best player that day was Marián Hossa. But he was born in 1979, so he wasn't eligible for the draft."

Henry was there to see players who were eligible for the 1996 draft. This big, six-foot, nine-inch defenceman that Routa was talking about, this Chára kid, had actually been passed over in his first year of NHL draft eligibility in 1995. "He wasn't picked in the draft the year before because they couldn't find skates big enough to fit him."

So, with the viewing of Hossa on the first day of this trip out of the way, Henry set his sights on Chára. There was another slew of games on the docket, and he showed up at the rink at ten to five. There was a massive lineup to get into the building. Paul Henry did what all great scouts do: He ran up to the door and pulled out his NHL card. The man at the door was not impressed with whatever type of foreign document this NHL scout was showing him. "He gave me eighteen '*nyets*.'"

Henry wanted in. He needed to see Chára. He did what any other crazed hockey fan would do. He went with profanity. "I said, 'This pass works in every fucking rink in the world,' and I just barrelled on in and I never missed a Chára shift."

Henry only had one problem. This was the first time he was seeing Chára. But it was also to be the only time he would see Chára. "I only saw him that one time, and I didn't have the balls to pick him in the first round, even though I absolutely loved him. He was doing Serge Savard spinaramas. He was ridiculous. But to draft a guy like that, only seeing him once, it was too tough."

Remember, Chára had gone undrafted the previous year, so to take him in the first round would have been a giant leap for a scout who had only seen him once. "We went to the finals [in 1996] with the Florida Panthers, and [at the trade deadline we'd given] San Jose our second-round pick for eighty-one-goal-scoring OHL star Ray Sheppard. He got us to the finals, but it cost us Chára because we would've picked him in the second round. And four picks from us in the third round, Anders Kallur, who won four Stanley Cup with the Islanders, he picked Chára. Only four picks before we were going to pick him."

Henry is quick to add that Kallur "has the record per capita for the fewest games with the most Cups." Part of the Islanders dynasty, he became a European scout for the team. And with the fifty-sixth pick, he landed Chára for the Islanders. No one picked in the 1996 draft played more NHL games than Zdeno Chára: an incredible 1,680 regular-season games and another two hundred in the playoffs, where he won a Stanley Cup with the Boston Bruins.

Henry eventually worked his way up to director of player development with the Panthers before he joined the Phoenix Coyotes' scouting staff. Then it was overseas to join Pierre Pagé with Red Bull Hockey in Germany and Austria. "I was lucky I watched a lot of European hockey, and that's what got me started working for Halifax," Henry says.

The Halifax Mooseheads won the Memorial Cup in 2013. They were loaded up front with talent like Nathan MacKinnon and Jonathan Drouin. In junior hockey, when you win, you often pay the price the following year. A lot of your top talent will move on. Teams at this level have to rebuild and reload. That can often be painful. That's when Henry entered the equation in Halifax. The Mooseheads had started to look to the future before they even hoisted the Memorial Cup.

"[Former Mooseheads owner] Bobby Smith hired Paul during the season that we won the Memorial Cup," says Cam Russell. "We just felt we needed a little more help with the European draft, so we brought Paul in partway through that season. He had worked as an amateur scout for Bobby in Phoenix [Smith had been GM of the Coyotes] and that's how Bobby had the connection," says Cam Russell.

Henry got right to work. And it is the way that he goes about his work that makes him stand out from the crowd—in the stands, in talks with the players, even in the airport. "My first trip to Europe with him, I had a nice suitcase with rolling wheels. And Paul showed up with his Jofa gear bag, which I ended up carrying around for him," says Russell.

"It's a *Warrior* hockey bag," Henry emphasizes. "When you're gone for three weeks, you need a hockey bag."

"He does not move quick," Russell says. "He stops and talks to everybody. He has to sample every food on the street, in the airport, or wherever he is. He is enjoying the culture. He is enjoying every bit of our trips. I spend my whole time going, 'Paul, let's go! Let's go!' I'm the impatient one. He's the guy that stops and enjoys the moment."

Henry takes his time when it comes to scouting, too. In a word, he is detailed. Very detailed, says Russell, and not just about what he sees on the ice.

"He scouts from puck drop to the end of the game. He does not leave early. He looks for parents to talk to. He searches out the moms and the dads. He has in-depth conversations with them. He has got time for everyone. When the kids first meet him, you know, they're a little apprehensive because he's a little off the wall, but as the conversation goes on, they just fall in love with the guy."

In his first year scouting for the Mooseheads, Paul helped them select Nikolaj Ehlers with the sixth pick in the Canadian Hockey League Import Draft. When Ehlers is mentioned, Paul doesn't hesitate before saying, "The best two performances I ever saw in junior hockey: John Tavares beat Belleville, 5–4. John had four goals and one assist. I never saw a junior ever play a game like that in all my years of scouting. He scored shorthanded, even strength.

"The second-best game I ever saw," he continued, "was Nikolaj

Ehlers. It was in Rouyn-Noranda, Quebec, Dave Keon Arena. Halifax was down 6–2. Nikolaj Ehlers took the game into his own hands—8–6 was the final for Halifax, three goals and three assists for Ehlers. I told Nik about that game years later and he said, 'No, no. It was four and two.'"

Henry helped Halifax get another gem, another future NHL star, with the twelfth pick in that same draft: Timo Meier. Remember how Russell pointed out that Henry doesn't just scout the games, that he wants to meet everyone in the arena? One night, he met Mr. Meier. "His dad told me that when Timo was ten years old, he was the best skier in Switzerland as well as the best ten-year-old hockey player in the country. So, he had to make a decision at the age of ten: hockey or skiing. Timo is a spectacular leader and human being."

About seven years after Timo made the choice to concentrate on hockey, he caught Henry's eye. As Henry says, he does not find players. The players find him. "I decided to go to Switzerland to see a Czech team. There was a boy who became a second-round pick with Buffalo who I was looking at. I went to see two other Czech players. I found two games in Lenzerheide, Switzerland. I had never been there before or after. And I still couldn't even tell you where the hell it is."

It was, it turns out, the place where Henry discovered a future NHL star and a kid who would one day become the high-scoring captain of the Halifax Mooseheads. "I went to watch these two players Friday night. The Czech team won, 4–0, and these two players I was going to draft for Halifax both got two and two, but the best player on the ice was a Swiss-born guy by the name of Timo Meier. He got stoned by the Czech goalie, who stood on his head that night. I went back the next day—Timo's team won, 3–2. He scored shorthanded, on a power play and at even strength. He single-handedly dismantled the Czech team."

Henry went a perfect two-for-two in his first import draft with the Mooseheads. Over the years, he has also helped bring players Nico Hischier, the number one pick in the 2017 NHL draft, to Halifax. "He is definitely one of a kind," says Russell. "He is a psychologist. He understands people. Hockey, it's an emotional roller coaster. The highs are super high, and the lows are super low. Paul is one of these guys that always makes you feel good about yourself. You will see him in the morning, and the first thing he will remark on is what a great jacket you have. 'Geez, that's a nice jacket. Where did you get that jacket?' Paul quietly makes you feel good about yourself, and you don't even realize that he's doing it. You always walk away feeling better about yourself when you've had a run-in with Paul Henry."

What does Henry look for in a player? "Class," he says. "The Draper brothers [Dave and Bruce] taught me everything I know. And if I don't know anything, it's the Draper brothers' fault. They were my mentors. We went to the same grade school. They were my big brothers."

Henry adds, "It's all about sharing and caring. Sharing and caring is so important."

To prove this point, Henry brings up the story about Trevor Stienburg—or rather, Trevor Stienburg's father, Mac. Trevor, a hockey lifer, was selected fifteenth overall by the Quebec Nordiques in 1984. He ended up playing seventy-one games in the NHL. He is currently a scout for the Seattle Kraken. Stienburg grew up in Moscow, Ontario, not far from Kingston, the same town where Henry worked at the Penn. Trevor's dad, the Reverend Malcolm "Mac" Stienburg, served as a parole officer. One of his parolees, Steven Truscott, who was convicted of murder in 1959, lived with the Stienburg family after he was paroled. He lived in the same home as young Trevor. "I learned a lot from Mac," says Henry. "Steven Truscott . . .

it was the most sensational case in 1959, and then Mac took Steven home on parole. To Trevor, he was Uncle Steven. Trevor coached twenty-five years at St. Mary's University, and now he scouts for Seattle. Mac had passion. Trevor had passion. Mac shared with me Trevor's passion, and that's etched in my mind."

Mac Stienburg saw the character that Steven Truscott had. Almost fifty years after he was convicted of murder, the Ontario Court of Appeal acquitted Truscott. They called his conviction "a miscarriage of justice." Stienburg saw something in Truscott that no one else did.

Trevor Stienburg shared the same passion—or perhaps, compassion—as his father. Mike Danton, formerly Mike Jefferson, who was convicted and served time for conspiracy to commit murder, ended up playing for Trevor Stienburg at St. Mary's, where he won a national championship in 2010. "If you don't care and you don't have passion, you got shit," says Henry. "Oh, and I saw Trevor's kid Matt play with the Colorado Eagles in Calgary back in November."

So, how long does Paul Henry plan on scouting, on fuelling his passion? Why is he still doing it?

"Why am I still doing it? Why? Because I'm still six years old? I have the same passion as I had when I was six."

Acknowledgements

A book like this does not happen without the people who agree to be a part of it, so first and foremost I would like to say a tremendous thank you to all the scouts who made this book possible. I can't thank you enough for sharing your time, stories and wisdom.

Thank you, Kevin Hanson, for the gift of your idea. Kevin came up with the idea for this book. Thanks for trusting me with it.

A massive thank you to everyone at Simon & Schuster, especially my editor, Jim Gifford. Sure, I will admit from time to time I can weave a tale, but I can't type and my grammar is horrible. Thank you for cleaning these pages up and turning my ramblings into a fantastic book.

To my agent, Brian Wood, for his continuous work. This is now our eighth book together. Thank you for always being open to my ideas and for your patience and understanding of the creative process.

I would like to thank "all the guys at work" for their support of my writing. Jon Coleman, Rob Corte, Mike Futa, Ryan Moynes, Evanka Osmak, Tim Micallef and many others have always had my back and have helped me promote my writing in countless ways.

So many people helped with suggestions and recommendations on who to talk to and helped point me in the right direction for this project. Thank you to Cam Russell, Allie MacDonald, Adam

Binkley, Paul Murray, Troy Shanks, Scott Landry, Darren Burns, Cassie Campbell-Pascall, Wayne Mundey, Michel Goulet, Ryan Cousins, Matt Marchese, Mac Templeton, Cleo, Craig Clarke, Gary Knickle, Mark Spector, Neil Hope, the *legend* Doug MacLean, Colby Armstrong, Dr. Grant Roberts, Robert Joseph Bass III, Gair Maxwell, Terry Ryan, Terry Ryan Sr. and Jesse Duke.

This book would also not be possible without the incredible amount of information available at eliteprospects.com, hockeydb.com, sihrhockey.org, hockey-reference.com and newspapers.com.

To my mom and dad, who planted the love of hockey in me—it didn't pay off on the ice, but it still worked out. To my brother, Peter, and sister, Katie, thanks for playing road hockey with me, especially Kate, who sometimes had to wear an XL7 and jump between the pipes.

And to my wife, Mrs. Reid, who totally gets it. Who lets me obsess over the game and share my love of all things hockey with our beautiful boys, Cobs and Lou.

And Cobs and Lou, thanks for making me smile every day.